IN TIMES OF CRISIS
U.S.-Japan Civil-Military Disaster Relief Coordination

James L. Schoff and Marina Travayiakis

T0323834

A Publication by
The Institute for Foreign Policy Analysis, Inc.

In Association with The Fletcher School, Tufts University

2009

Potomac Books, Inc.

(Editorial)   22841 Quicksilver Dr., Dulles, Virginia 20166 USA

(Orders)   Potomac Book Orders, P.O. Box 960, Herndon, Virginia 22070 USA

Copyright©2009 Potomac Books, Inc.

Brassey's books are available at special discounts for bulk purchases for sales, promotions, premiums, fundraising, or educational use.

Library of Congress Cataloging-in-Publication Data

In times of crisis

ISBN: 978-1-59797-406-6. $25.00

CIP information not ready at time of publication

Designed by J. Christian Hoffman

Printed in the United States of America by Universal Millennium Press, Westwood, Massachusetts

10 9 8 7 6 5 4 3 2 1

CONTENTS

Introduction and Acknowledgements

The succession of large-scale natural disasters and ambitious nation-building projects that have occurred or have been undertaken globally in the last several years has focused attention on the potential value of deploying national military assets in support of disaster relief and recovery efforts, as well as on the challenges that international disaster relief agencies and nongovernmental organizations (NGOs) face when working closely with dispatched military units. In the United States, this has led to a serious discussion in government circles about possible ways to adjust the military structure and training regimen in order to enhance the military's effectiveness in certain complex or catastrophic cases, including the development of a dedicated response capability and the enhancement of joint planning or training with non-military groups.

The goal of these adjustments is relatively straightforward: to improve U.S. government and military readiness for domestic or overseas relief missions to which Washington will inevitably be called on to contribute. The motivation behind this goal, however, is more complex, especially when it comes to overseas operations, since it is recognized that such missions are increasingly connected to national security and diplomatic objectives. For similar reasons, Japan is examining ways that its civil society and military sectors can contribute more directly to disaster relief efforts and so-called international peace cooperation activities, making this an important time to foster dialogue and cross-fertilization of related ideas and initiatives between the two allies and beyond.

Both U.S. and Japanese policy makers understand that leveraging military resources in times of crisis is first and foremost an opportunity to do good, to save lives and property, and to help maintain stability and prosperity in affected communities and nations. This is particularly true in the wake of catastrophic disasters that quickly overwhelm the response capabilities of the affected nation and the international organizations it reaches out to for assistance. But Washington policy makers in particular recognize that responding effectively can further U.S. foreign policy goals by helping to eliminate sources of instability, building or restoring cooperative military ties with host and contributing nations that can prove useful in other mission areas, and establishing goodwill in countries where it has been latent at best. This was at least a small part of the U.S. government's calculation when it responded ardently to the 2004 Indian Ocean tsunami, the 2005 Pakistan earthquake, the 2006 Philippines mudslides, the 2008 cyclone disaster in Burma (Myanmar), and the catastrophic earthquake in Sichuan, China that same year. Moreover, a failure to respond adequately can be devastating to the affected communities and will inevitably lead to charges of abandonment, indifference, and isolation on the part of America and its allies, which can undermine their interests and international cooperation more broadly.

For all of these reasons, U.S. policy makers are seeking to strengthen America's contributions to international disaster relief efforts, and they cannot ignore the attention being given to enhancing civil-military coordination (CMCoord) for these operations. It is quite clear that international military involvement in relief operations has saved countless lives in recent years, and it is not unreasonable to expect that strengthening CMCoord could further improve response to large-scale disasters. This experience also demonstrates, however, that many organizational, legal, and cultural obstacles can impede cooperation among the many actors who respond to a crisis, preventing the full realization of this CMCoord potential. The challenges are numerous and include command and control issues, information sharing, and field coordination.

In addition, U.S. civilian and military officials have given mixed signals regarding their intentions and motivations, with some more focused on the "do good" opportunity in disaster relief missions, while others suggest a broader interest in Washington for strengthening CMCoord in support of diplomatic objectives (or even force protection), particularly when this involves so-called stability operations in places like Iraq and Afghanistan. These signals have led to worry by some at the United Nations (UN) and among NGOs that the United States is politicizing CMCoord and potentially threatening their impartiality in volatile areas.

In Japan, the discussion regarding CMCoord has not developed as far as it has in the United States, but this situation is changing as Japanese NGOs and Japan's self-defense forces (SDF) expand their involvement in disaster relief and international peace and reconstruction activities, as they did for the tsunami relief effort and the Pakistan earthquake, as well as in Afghanistan and Iraq. New NGOs are being formed in Japan that are specifically designed to provide assistance to these kinds of operations.[1] Japan's National Defense Program Guideline (NDPG) for FY 2005 and After paved the way for the country to become more proactive in overseas emergency assistance and peace cooperation activities, supported by new procurements, training programs, and a joint command structure formed in 2006. This culminated in early 2007, when Japan's Defense Agency was upgraded to a full ministry, and overseas missions became primary duties of the new ministry, as opposed to secondary.[2] Japan's new NDPG in 2009 is expected to build upon this trend.

To support these changes, several Japanese government agencies and universities have launched studies of CMCoord, and these organizations have been cooperating with the United States bilaterally and within multilateral frameworks through various workshops, seminars, and tabletop exercises. Although public support in Japan for the SDF's participation in international disaster relief missions has increased in the last ten to fifteen years, disagreement remains within the government and among civil society about how extensive the SDF's involvement should be. Japan is interested in joining the CMCoord debate to enhance its own understanding of the issues and to contribute to improving cooperation with the United States in ways that strengthen its own civilian and military institutions.

Of course, the debate about enhancing CMCoord is not limited to Washington and Tokyo, as this is truly a global phenomenon driven by

---

1   These include Japan Mine Action Service in 2002 and Engineers without Borders in 2005.

2   These changes were accomplished by passage of the Law Concerning Partial Amendment of the Establishment of the Defense Agency on December 15, 2006.

the combination of persistent human vulnerability and a greater technical and financial capacity on the part of wealthy nations to respond. This response capacity, however, is not centralized, so large-scale disaster relief missions are often conducted by loose, ad hoc coalitions of international organizations, NGOs, and national aid agencies and militaries, as opposed to being managed almost exclusively by the UN and its affiliated agencies and organizations. This arrangement places a premium on nation-to-nation communication and cooperation during a crisis, even though these networks are not fully developed.

CMCoord and related policies are therefore at a critical stage in the United States and Japan, as well as in the international community. Success in these efforts can contribute not only to more effective relief and recovery operations, but also to greater interaction and mutual understanding among national militaries and the NGO community. Further, effective CMCoord can strengthen international and regional organizations by giving them access to more synergistic civil-military coalitions. The United States and Japan are by no means the only two countries engaged in this effort, but they can play a unique role by virtue of their financial power (in terms of their contributions to the UN and other international organizations, and direct overseas development assistance) and their strong security relationship, which features frequent joint training opportunities and a high degree of interoperability.

Together with a handful of other key countries in Europe and East Asia, the United States and Japan can help form a valuable crisis core group that cooperates in support of large-scale, UN-led disaster relief operations. This kind of core group (of perhaps four to six nations) is generally more effective at making decisions and harmonizing policies and procedures than either a large collection of dozens of countries or uncoordinated efforts by individual countries, and it could play an invaluable support role to the UN or to host nations in the early days following a disaster. An important part of making this core-group idea work, however, is achieving greater mutual awareness and understanding about these issues among a wide variety of policy makers, military officials, and academics in the United States and Japan, which is a primary objective of the research and dialogue project described in this report.

Our project focused on improving the ability of the United States and Japan to effectively pool civilian and military resources and to respond together (bilaterally or as part of a broader coalition) in support of host nations and international relief agencies to alleviate suffering and to speed recovery in a time of crisis. Indeed, it is the pressure of time (an integral part of any crisis) that underscores the value of extensive dialogue and preparation in advance of a coordinated response to a natural or man-made disaster. The ability to respond in a timely fashion requires an ongoing regimen of effective planning and communication, which in turn relies on strong personal and institutional relationships between the two countries and with other partners. Our project sought to strengthen and diversify these relationships with the aim of helping the individuals and organizations involved to be better prepared, to respond more efficiently, and to improve over time as they incorporate lessons from shared experiences.

The In Times of Crisis project was a multi-year joint effort of the Institute for Foreign Policy Analysis (IFPA) and the Osaka School of International Public Policy (OSIPP) at Osaka University, together with a number of individual scholars in Japan. Project team members examined both domestic and international characteristics of the CMCoord debate from the two countries' points of view, in order to explain how CMCoord is developing in each country, as well as how each country (or various institutions within the country) views international CMCoord developments and how they relate to their participation in future multilateral operations. The project team's goal was to build linkages between the two countries across the spectrum of NGOs, government officials, scholars, and military officers. In addition to archival research and one-on-one interviews, the team organized a day-long bilateral workshop in Washington, D.C., on December 12, 2006, and another in Tokyo on October 28, 2008, that brought together government and military officials from relevant agencies, along with UN officials and American and Japanese NGOs, and policy specialists to discuss these issues.

This report generally draws a distinction between CMCoord for disaster relief operations and CMCoord for stabilization and reconstruction missions (such as in Afghanistan and Iraq). Part of the reason for this distinction is the fact that some real differences exist between the two types of missions, in terms of the kinds of activities carried out by the responding organizations, the speed with which the activities are carried out, and the overall environment in which they operate. It is also true that stability operations are much more political and controversial by nature, and there are a number of legal questions regarding how involved Japan's SDF can be in certain dangerous situations. That said, the personal networks, communications infrastructure, and many key capabilities and operating procedures often apply to both types of CMCoord, so it is neither practical nor advisable to ignore stabilization/reconstruction situations altogether. Therefore, while the IFPA-OSIPP project focused primarily on CMCoord in disaster relief and consequence management situations, some mention of stabilization/reconstruction CMCoord issues is unavoidable. This report details the key findings from the project, and it serves as a primer for CMCoord in the two countries and related policy reforms. The report also identifies the most promising areas for bilateral cooperation within international frameworks.

The authors are grateful to key members of the project team for their contributions to this project to date: Dr. Hoshino Toshiya (OSIPP), Dr. Robert Eldridge (OSIPP), Dr. Atsumi Tomohide (Osaka University), Dr. Yoshizaki Tomonori (Japan's National Institute for Defense Studies), Dr. Nagamatsu Shingo (then at the Disaster Reduction & Human Renovation Institution), Dr. Uesugi Yuji (Hiroshima University), and Dr. Charles M. Perry and RADM (Ret.) Eric A. McVadon USN of IFPA. The authors also thank the officials and specialists who have given their time in interviews and through presentations or comments at the workshops, in particular those who serve as unofficial advisors to the project, including Ms. Nancy Lindborg (Mercy Corps), Ms. Linda Poteat (InterAction), Ms. Seki Kaoruko (UN-OCHA), Mr. Rabih Torbay (International Medical Corps), Ms. Yamamoto Rika (Peace Winds Japan), and Mr. Takamatsu Koji (then of Japan Platform). Other specialists, officials, and military officers who generously gave of their time and expertise in interviews and workshops include Chuck Aanenson, Tom Baltazar, Samina Bhatia, Leo Bosner, Pete Bradford, James Castle, Steve Catlin, Kathleen Connolly, Tom Dolan, Paul Fujimura, Lt Gen (Ret.) W.C. "Chip" Gregson USMC, Brian Grzelkowski, Bailey Hand, Lt. General Hayashi Kazuya JGSDF, Hayashi Ryoji, Heff Hensel, Colonel Hiroe Jiro JGSDF, Horie Yoshiteru, Colonel Horikiri Mitsuhiko JGSDF, Major General Isobe Koichi JGSDF, Iwasaki Naoko, Lt. Col. Brett Jackman USMC, Vice Admiral Kaneda Hideaki JMSDF, Kawakami Takashi, Brendan Kearney, Kiyama Keiko, Colonel Kudo Takahiko JGSDF, Kuwana Megumi, James Lawler, Simon Lee, Rear

Admiral Michael LeFever USN, Kate Stone Legates, Colonel Mark Losack USMC, Marui Kentaro, Matsumoto Sayaka, Matsuura Misaki, Mikami Emiko, Douglas Meffert, Gary Oba, Ohue Hirofumi, Colonel Okimura Yoshihiko JGSDF, Barry Pavel, Allan Reed, Scott Rolston, Sano Hiroaki, Sato Masaru, Colonel Shigemura Kazuyuki JGSDF, Shiina Noriyuki, Ken Staley, Rob Thayer, Tokuchi Hideshi, Phil Wilhelm, Colonel Jeffrey Wiltse USA, Lt. General (Ret.) Yamaguchi Noboru JGSDF, Lt. Colonel Yamamoto Yutaka JGSDF, Yamanouchi Kanji, and Yokoi Yutaka. Valuable assistance at IFPA came from Nakai Aki, Charles Lister, and Koga Kei (research), Adelaide Ketchum (editing), and Christian Hoffman (graphic art and publication design). The entire project team is grateful to the Japan Foundation's Center for Global Partnership (CGP) for its financial support, advice, and encouragement throughout this entire project. In this report, Japanese names appear with the family name first and the given name second, as is the Japanese custom.

Executive Summary

The United States and Japan are seeking to strengthen their countries' contributions to international disaster relief efforts, and they cannot ignore the value that civil-military coordination (CMCoord) brings to these operations. International military involvement in relief operations has saved countless lives in recent years, and strengthening CMCoord could further improve responses to large-scale disasters. This experience also demonstrates, however, that organizational, legal, and cultural obstacles impede cooperation among the many actors who respond to a crisis, preventing the full realization of this CMCoord potential. The challenges are numerous and include command and control issues, information sharing, and field coordination. In addition, military support for disaster relief operations and related missions should not encroach upon the humanitarian space occupied by NGOs, UN agencies, and civilian government organs that are the primary tools to aid communities and nations in times of crisis.

CMCoord and related policies are at an important stage, and improvement in this area can contribute not only to more effective relief and recovery operations, but also to greater interaction and mutual understanding among national militaries and the NGO community. Further, effective CMCoord can strengthen international and regional organizations by giving them access to more synergistic civil-military coalitions. The United States and Japan are not the only two countries engaged in this effort, but they can play a unique role by virtue of their financial power (in terms of contributions to the UN and other international organizations, and direct overseas development assistance) and their strong security relationship, which features frequent joint training exercises and a high degree of interoperability. U.S.-Japan CMCoord can create opportunities to contribute to global stability and prosperity, and at the same time it can strengthen the alliance relationship in a variety of ways that will prepare them for other important missions.

U.S.-Japan bilateral cooperation on these issues (together with other partners in the region) can help build more diverse and sophisticated alliance relationships that bring together a wider range of ministries, departments, and agencies to address common challenges of all types. This will ultimately serve to improve the ability of the alliance to work with other countries on these issues through multilateral initiatives and with international organizations. Enhancing CMCoord for disaster relief operations is a beneficial alliance exercise because:

- CMCoord is useful
- The need for CMCoord is constant
- CMCoord is inherently an interagency or "whole-of-government" responsibility in collaboration with NGOs and international bodies (so it "exercises" these increasingly important alliance "muscles" that can be valuable in a variety of regional contingencies)
- CMCoord is "exportable": it can help protect the homeland and third countries overseas, contributing to regional stability and multilateral security cooperation
- CMCoord is not politically controversial

The United States and Japan approach the CMCoord issue from different positions of strength and experience. The U.S. military is well funded and extremely capable, but it has been drawn into the disaster relief role in recent years at times reluctantly, given the combat and counter-insurgency demands it has faced since 2001. Japan's SDF has a very high tempo of domestic relief operations, but it has relatively little experience overseas and limited projection capability. U.S. NGOs are better funded and have more international experience than their Japanese counterparts, but in Asia Japan's NGOs often have complementary networks of local staff and technical expertise. Moreover, Japan's disaster relief teams can be a valuable asset.

Core Crisis Group

Together with a handful of other key countries in Europe and East Asia, the United States and Japan can help form a valuable core crisis group that cooperates in support of large-scale, UN-led disaster relief operations. This kind of core group (of perhaps four to six nations) is generally more effective at making decisions and harmonizing policies and procedures than either a large collection of dozens of countries or uncoordinated efforts by individual countries, and it could provide invaluable support to the UN or to host nations in the early days following a disaster.

Maintaining CMCoord

Thinking about and taking steps to maintain CMCoord across the lifecycle of an event —from first response to last act of assistance —remains central to the concept of continuous operations that is so vital to a well-managed relief effort, since it is the military sprinters who buy the time that the civilian marathoners need to fully mobilize and eventually assume command in the recovery and reconstruction phase of an HA/DR operation.

It is probably too difficult (and unnecessary) to try to bridge the gaps between the military and civilian sectors for disaster relief situations in a comprehensive way. In other words, U.S.-Japan military-to-military interactions and parallel civilian-to-civilian interactions are likely to be much more productive than trying to integrate civil-military dialogues and policies across the alliance with any sort of regularity.

Of course, these parallel civilian and military interactions need to be connected to each other in some way in order to set complementary goals and maintain communication and mutual awareness as they progress, but it is not necessary to impose common CMCoord solutions on the alliance. In this sense, American CMCoord and Japanese CMCoord will be like two different doors that open with their own key, but there should be a master key that can work both doors when the need arises. Developing this link between the two, in conjunction with the UN and other partners in the region, is a prime objective.

Overall, this linkage and these interactions should focus most on planning, preparation, communication, and assessment issues related to disaster relief, since actual operations are more likely to be carried out separately by U.S. and Japanese forces and civilian teams. Promoting joint U.S.-Japan disaster relief operations, therefore, should not be a specific goal of alliance managers, but more efficient and productive coordination of U.S. and Japanese contributions to these multinational operations is a worthwhile objective. This can start at the far end of the preparation and planning spectrum, including coordinated disaster reduction and capacity building through development assistance to disaster-prone countries, as well as adjusting (or perhaps adding to) pre-positioned stockpiles of disaster relief supplies throughout the region.

Bilateral cooperation in this area can also move into more detailed planning tasks by identifying complementary specialties or a viable division of labor in certain circumstances, standardizing information flows (such as scripting requests for assistance and collaborating on advance contracting arrangements), and harmonizing damage- and needs-assessment procedures.

Increasingly this kind of so-called theater security cooperation (TSC) involves more than just two allies working together, as shared interests in regional stability, open trade, anti-piracy and counterterrorism, disaster relief, and similar objectives are prompting more frequent collaboration amongst a wider variety of increasingly capable players. These joint exercises can include, it is worth noting, the construction of warehouses, supply depots, airstrips, and port facilities to which the allies might be granted access during future contingencies (as a part of "exercise-related construction").

The budgets supporting TSC and related training activities are relatively modest, however, and TSC is often perceived as competition for "real" needs. This kind of joint training, however, is an important part of training forces to conduct military operations in the challenging environment of coalition politics. At the tactical and operational level, knowing how to work with forces from different cultural backgrounds and different doctrinal schools is critically important and difficult to learn from a book (interview 2004). The value of these training investments can be enhanced through more effective and timely coordination between the military and civilian officials and specialists.

Cataloguing Assets, Roles, and Resources

Another step in improving the ability of the United States and Japan to effectively pool their civilian and military resources in response to humanitarian crises is to identify and catalogue what assets (civil and military personnel, material and equipment, and support assets) are available to each country for HA/DR activities, particularly in Asia. This process should help familiarize U.S. and Japanese officials with one another's capacities to respond to a crisis, without necessarily committing either party to exchange logistics support and services. This exercise could also go beyond pinpointing available military assets, such as heavy-lift helicopters, naval vessels, and surveillance equipment, to reach into private-sector and NGO capabilities. Private-sector capabilities are particularly well suited to the areas of communication, damage assessment (involving commercial satellites and local NGO staff), and transportation.

Understanding the roles and resources of each actor involved in disaster relief creates familiarity at the strategic and operational levels of a mission, as well as helping to identify critical gaps in each country's disaster response capacities. In time, this process may lead to the development of a disaster management database, similar to OCHA's Central Register of Disaster Management Capacities. A bilateral inventory list specifying the civilian and military assets, support services, and personnel available for or, at minimum, trained for complex emergencies could enhance the capacity of the United States and Japan to respond, either alone or together, to an emerging crisis. Exchanging information on the availability of military assets would also help U.S. and Japanese planning efforts. But a bilateral effort in this area should be well coordinated with OCHA and other regional efforts, such as the contact points for the disaster relief database compiled by the ASEAN Regional Forum (ARF). Databases such as these are notorious for becoming quickly outdated and inaccurate, and there is significant room to improve database development and management; this could be a productive area for enhancing efficiency through bilateral cooperation within multilateral frameworks.

Mutual Assistance and Support Agreements
Another means to improve government and military relations with NGOs and the private sector, as well as to enhance U.S.-Japan cooperation overall, is the establishment of mutual assistance and support agreements, or memorandums of understanding (MOUs), for disaster re-

lief operations. The current U.S.-Japan Acquisition and Cross-Servicing Agreement enables U.S. and Japanese forces to provide mutual logistics support, exchange supplies—including food and fuel—and use each other's transportation and communications equipment, for reimbursement either in cash, replacement in kind, or equal value exchange. But the potential applicability of this agreement is not well understood in the broader disaster relief community, and although it can be used in disaster relief situations, it is not specifically designed to do so.

In addition to military-to-military MOUs, the two countries might study the benefits of signing MOUs with humanitarian and private-sector organizations. UN agencies, for example, have signed MOUs with several NGO and private-sector organizations, such as the International Federation of the Red Cross and Red Crescent Societies, OXFAM GB, and Deutsche Post World Net, the parent company of DHL, an international express and logistics company.

Standby arrangements for disaster management and emergency response between U.S. and Japanese civil and military partners would also enhance the ability of the two countries to mobilize resources quickly. A standby arrangement would commit each party to maintain specified resources on standby, such as technical and logistics resources, field staff, and material and equipment. Joint capacity-mapping exercises could help identify the allies' strengths and weaknesses, reveal which areas require additional investment, in terms of resources, personnel, and training, as well as determine which assets U.S. and Japanese forces should make available to one another to avoid duplications in assistance efforts. Moreover, this process could identify how best to integrate the UN, NGOs, and private-sector companies into disaster preparedness plans and relief efforts.

For now, standby arrangements for military capabilities might be difficult to implement, but introducing bilateral standby arrangements between U.S. and Japanese government agencies, NGOs, and private-sector companies is more feasible. OCHA has had in place standby arrangements with governments and humanitarian organizations for the provision of emergency staff and equipment during disasters, and the UN Department of Peacekeeping has in place a similar arrangement, the UN Stand-by Arrangement System (UNSAS). Forums in East

Asia have proposed establishing similar arrangements for regional disaster response and humanitarian activities, but the degree of U.S. and Japanese involvement in these programs has been limited, and neither is well aware of the other's national agreements, such as they are. The allies could compare and, when appropriate, further develop bilateral standby arrangements with relief agencies and commercial aircraft carriers and shipping companies, with an eye toward establishing an element of reciprocity with each other and perhaps with other nations and organizations.

Information Management

Information management is an overriding challenge for CMCoord, though this seemingly simple objective can mean slightly different things to different stakeholders. For many at OCHA, greater standardization of how information is provided by and managed among crisis response partners is the top priority for improving CMCoord. From their perspective, this includes information about the availability and capability of certain assets or personnel, the terms of their deployment, standardization of assessment reports and procedures, and a high degree of interoperability among the contributing organizations and governments.

For some this is a process of developing compatible systems, but others might emphasize training people to understand different responding organizations' capabilities and how they operate. Still others take this a step further and emphasize the personal relationships among responders in the field as the key factor. All of these perspectives are valid, but each of them suggests a slightly different focus for CMCoord training and cooperation in a bilateral (or mini-lateral) context.[1] Developing practical options to increase and strengthen U.S.-Japan peer-to-peer interactions on CMCoord issues, while maintaining connections between these groups, should help the two countries to clarify how they can best contribute to the process of CMCoord improvement.

---

1   The term "mini-lateral" refers to multilateral activities with relatively few players (usually just three or four), as a way to differentiate from larger multilateral initiatives involving many more countries.

Conclusion

Overall, strengthening the U.S.-Japan alliance for disaster response may increase the two countries' participation in regional and multilateral HA/DR missions, which will be a good thing for affected nations and for the alliance. Harmonizing policies and procedures among close allies would improve how they cooperate together or as members of a coalition, as well as pave the way for achieving a more efficient international framework for disaster response and recovery. Finally, opportunities for enhanced U.S.-Japan civil-military cooperation in disaster management and emergency response can serve as a catalyst for greater cooperation throughout the Asia-Pacific region for missions such as peacekeeping, counterproliferation, counterterrorism, and maritime security.

Understanding the Civil-Military Coordination Issue

Coordinating the civilian and military components of international humanitarian assistance/disaster relief (HA/DR) activities is not a new undertaking, and it has always been a difficult challenge. The increased frequency and large scale of these combined operations, together with their potential positive impact if done well are bringing renewed attention to ways to improve. Even when they are carrying out roughly the same mission, the NGO and military communities have very different cultures and priorities, they operate under different codes of conduct (or rules of engagement) and with different organizational philosophies, and they are subject to different types of international law. This is evident at the most basic level on the question of how even to refer to CMCoord. The United Nations prefers the term "CMCoord" (civil-military *coordination*), which has a slightly more detached connotation than *cooperation* (as in civil-military cooperation, or CIMIC, often used by the North Atlantic Treaty Organization (NATO)). "CMCoord" paints a far more neutral image than the oft-used U.S. military acronym CMO (or civil-military *operations*). However the UN term is not detached enough for some NGOs that want to avoid any connotation of collaboration and coordination and who instead prefer the term civil-military *relations*. For these NGOs, the use of the term "relations" better describes a simple state of coexistence or of (relatively) conflict-free actions in the field.

The CMCoord debate is driven above all by circumstances, however, and regardless of what one names the function, the need to address these CMCoord issues is clear to most parties involved, given the potential benefits of good coordination and the dangers of poor coordination. A UN-led group of NGOs and international organizations, for example, noted that because of the "changing nature of modern complex emergencies," the humanitarian community and non-UN militaries find themselves operating more closely together than ever before. "These developments, together with cases of military interventions claimed to be for 'humanitarian' purposes, have led to an erosion of the separation between the humanitarian and military space" (Inter-Agency Standing Committee 2004).

The concept of humanitarian space is important, and it does not refer to the physical space in which NGOs and UN agencies may operate. Instead, it refers to the complete freedom afforded to aid and relief workers to deliver assistance according to the three core humanitarian principles of humanity, neutrality, and impartiality (UN General Assembly 1991). Aid agencies and workers rely on this humanitarian space for their protection in areas of conflict, and they are sensitive to any potential damage to this metaphysical space caused by being too closely associated with a national military force.

Since the end of the Cold War, the United States, Europe, Japan, and a few other nations have been increasingly willing to use their militaries as a tool to help reduce conflict or alleviate suffering (compared to during the Cold War era, when the use of military assets by NATO or Warsaw Pact member countries created more strategic and geopolitical complications than is now usually the case). The relief operation Sea Angel (including many U.S. naval assets) in the aftermath of the 1991 catastrophic cyclone and flood in Bangladesh was one of the first such examples of dispatching the military to support relief operations. Operation Sea Angel was followed by operation Restore Hope in 1992, when a U.S.-led coalition of troops went to Somalia to protect relief workers and to help restore a major UN relief effort there. Similar operations have been (or are being) carried out in Haiti beginning in 1994, Bosnia in 1995, Kosovo in 1998, East Timor in 1999, and Afghanistan in 2001, along with other disaster relief activities that involved significant military deployments, such as after hurricane Mitch in Central America in 1998, and more recently the tsunami relief effort and the multilateral response following Pakistan's earthquake.

This phenomenon has caused military planners to adjust certain procurement and training strategies, and it has also confronted UN agency and NGO managers with new realities. As the scale and frequency of these combined operations increase, so too does the challenge to these managers in working alongside outside national militaries (usually referred to as "other deployed forces"), as opposed to affected-nation militaries or blue-helmeted UN peacekeepers. The NGO staffs are used to working in conflict areas and dangerous situations, but they could generally rely on their clear neutrality and impartiality (and UN mandate) for sufficient protection, and coordination was less complicated. Now they find themselves arguing with their national military counterparts as to how to assess need and priorities, the relative merits of a "demand pull" or "supply push" relief approach, whether or not the two groups can work together to distribute relief supplies or provide medical services, if the soldiers can wear civilian clothing, with side arms or without, and many other difficult questions. Coordination is particularly challenging, as other deployed forces frequently work directly with the affected nation's military outside of the UN's normal coordination circle.

In large-scale disaster relief operations, NGOs recognize the contributions made by these forces, but, as one NGO executive put it, they would generally prefer that these militaries restrict their role to providing infrastructure or logistical support and otherwise "leave the relief work to the professionals" (interview 2005). The soldiers, however, who are usually not specifically trained for these operations, tend to try to fill what they see as a leadership vacuum and seek to plug NGO resources and capabilities into their overall operation. Moreover, seemingly mundane issues of military contracting and cross-servicing, lines of command and communication, bureaucratic approvals, liability, and rules governing classified information and networks can frequently frustrate otherwise productive collaboration.

At the top of this scheme is the United Nations, which is supposed to coordinate all efforts (civilian and military) in support of the relief operation being led by the affected nation, yet this becomes extremely difficult when dozens of outside actors converge to assist relatively poor and unprepared nations that are overwhelmed by a large-scale disaster. Contributing governments and militaries all have different rules and procedures regarding how they interact with the UN and the affected nation, and they often seek distinct credit and acknowledgment for their efforts. One NGO field operator also noted, "Coordination is crucial...but you can literally spend all day [during a disaster] going from one coordination meeting to another and not get anything done. There are coordination meetings to coordinate the coordinators! So we've got to be smart about this" (IFPA-OSIPP 2006). The UN itself is sensitive to this situation and recognizes that organizations usually do not like to "be coordinated" in the sense that they are taking orders from the UN. This is why UN officials often stress that the UN "facilitates" coordination and that "coordination is not a function, but a shared responsibility" (IFPA-OSIPP 2006).

Despite the fact that officials and practitioners have been wrestling with a variety of CMCoord issues for several years, as well as benefiting from some well-documented experiences in the field, decision making in such a broad international forum is always difficult. Although some consensus has been reached on certain issues, even fundamental questions about what role military forces should be allowed or encouraged to play remain open. Just because the military *can* do something, for example, does not mean that it should. During one cleanup operation in Indonesia after the December 2004 tsunami, a group of NGOs were assisting local villagers with the labor-intensive process of separating wreckage piece by piece, creating piles of different materials that could be reused, recycled, burned, or discarded. The operation involved a large and diverse segment of the village population, creating a communal sense of rebuilding, and each worker earned a small wage that contributed wealth to his or her family. Within a few days, however, a military detail came in with heavy equipment, dug deep holes and pushed all the debris into large pits. The job was done much faster, but it proved to be more expensive (factoring in the cost to mobilize the men and equipment) and possibly undermined the village's rebuilding effort (interview 2006a).

In theory, military assistance is only to be sought as a last resort, when there is no other way to fill an identified need. But in practice, the assessment of needs and capabilities is often in the eye of the beholder. In the example above, was the need for speed more important to allow for a quicker reconstruction, or was a communal, wage-earning activity more helpful to the village? An argument could be made either way. Who makes the decision? Similar examples can be found in the aftermath of the 2005 Pakistan earthquake, such as the delivery and construction of local school buildings by U.S. forces, or even during domestic operations in Japan when SDF personnel delivered, cooked, and served the food for victims of the Niigata-Chuestsu earthquake in 2004, among other duties. For every person who expresses praise or thanks for such military contributions, one can usually find a critic who thinks that they go too far, especially when the military contribution involves the final stage of service delivery to the affected community (known as direct assistance) or continues for weeks or months after the initial disaster.

But few, if any, would deny that national militaries can provide critical support when responding to a large-scale natural disaster, whether it is the ability to organize quickly on the scene or to provide unrivaled logistical capabilities. During the Pakistan earthquake relief effort, for example, U.S. military helicopters carried more than twenty thousand passengers, conducted over thirty-seven hundred medical evacuations,

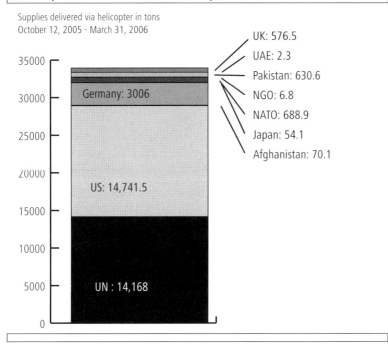

Total Tonnage of Relief Supplies Delivered in Response to the Pakistan Earthquake

Supplies delivered via helicopter in tons
October 12, 2005 - March 31, 2006

UK: 576.5
UAE: 2.3
Pakistan: 630.6
NGO: 6.8
NATO: 688.9
Japan: 54.1
Afghanistan: 70.1

Germany: 3006

US: 14,741.5

UN : 14,168

and delivered nearly fifteen thousand tons of cargo to distressed villages, which was more than any other country or organization handled, including the UN. Military units delivered fuel, serviced equipment, erected buildings, set up mobile hospitals, and provided medical care to more than forty thousand patients (IFPA-OSIPP 2006). Japan's SDF helicopters delivered over fifty-four tons of cargo during the Pakistan operation, part of a non-U.S., non-UN group of countries whose military hardware carried more than five thousand tons of relief supplies.

As one participant at the December 2006 workshop aptly put it, "The CMCoord debate often tries to bridge the most dramatic differences in our [NGO and military] approaches and priorities. The truth is, if you list up the ten most important objectives of the civilian and military sectors, we agree on six or seven of them. We're better off discussing those points of agreement, rather than focus on where we disagree" (IFPA-OSIPP 2006). In the end, it is clear that the question is not whether or not to involve the military in certain circumstances, but rather what is the right balance and how to manage that interaction. This is being considered in earnest in the United States and Japan.

In the United States in the 1990s, mobilizing the military to assist with disaster relief or stability operations overseas was generally seen as an anomaly. This attitude has gradually changed, however, for a variety of reasons. As noted earlier, it became politically and technologically easier to dispatch forces abroad for such missions after the Cold War ended, and the number and frequency of such operations increased. Later, the post-September 11 security environment forced U.S. military planners to expand their definition of an event with strategic implications. Moreover, while the Asia-Pacific region does play an increasingly important role in world trading, finance, and energy markets, its high population density and the severity of the disasters that hit the region can have disproportionately negative effects on local populations and global markets.[1] In addition, hurricanes Katrina and Rita in the United States in 2005 awakened U.S. officials to the inadequacies of their

---

1   It should be noted that this is not limited to natural disasters, as the SARS outbreak in Asia showed the potential human and financial cost of disease pandemics in the region, and more recently Japan's SDF and China's military (among others) were called on to help cull infected birds to help avoid an outbreak of pandemic influenza.

plans and preparations for responding to catastrophic domestic events, the list of which has grown since the government started factoring in potential terrorist attacks using weapons of mass destruction (WMDs). As a result, U.S. policy makers no longer see such scenarios and the capabilities needed to respond to them as unique or outside of their area of operations, and they are looking for ways to develop the necessary response skills.

The State Department, which takes the U.S. lead for assisting with disasters overseas, has worked to stay current with CMCoord developments. When the military started to get more involved in the 1990s, for example, the State Department's Agency for International Development (USAID) published a field operations guide for its assessment teams and disaster assistance response teams (DARTs) that included a chapter on working with U.S. military forces during relief activities. The field guide was updated in 2005 (USAID 2005), and it outlines the military's structure and roles during operations, and how, when, and where assessment teams and DARTs can coordinate the work of USAID's Office of U.S. Foreign Disaster Assistance (OFDA) with that of the military. As stability operations became more frequent, the U.S. government created the Office of the Coordinator for Reconstruction and Stabilization (S/CRS) in 2004. This new office within the State Department was charged with improving the working relationship between civilian agencies, the NGO community, and the military, and helping to prepare for and deal with post-conflict situations in places like Afghanistan and Iraq. More studies, reports, and recommendations soon followed.

The U.S. military also began to address these issues in earnest in the 1990s, with the Joint Chiefs of Staff, for example, producing its first manual on interagency coordination for joint operations in 1996. The purpose of that document was to establish doctrine and guidance for commanders who increasingly found themselves involved in "military operations other than war" (Joint Chiefs of Staff 1996). By the time the document was updated in 2006, it expanded beyond interagency coordination to include coordination with intergovernmental organizations and nongovernmental organizations (Joint Chiefs of Staff 2006). At about the same time, the Department of Defense (DoD) approved a new directive in December 2005 that elevates stability operations to a core military mission that "should be given priority comparable to combat operations (Department of Defense 2005). The directive instructs the Pentagon to "be prepared to work closely with relevant U.S. departments and agencies, foreign governments and security forces, global and regional international organizations, U.S. and foreign NGOs, and private-sector individuals and for-profit companies." Many of these capabilities and procedures will be applicable in support of large-scale disaster relief operations, not only overseas, but also domestically.

On this domestic front, the Pentagon has considered creating an active-duty force for responding to major natural disasters, in light of the lessons learned from hurricanes Katrina and Rita, though this has caused some consternation among state governors and NGOs such as the Red Cross (Tyson 2005). The assistant secretary of defense for homeland defense, Paul McHale, stressed that the response of active-duty troops would be limited to rare and massive catastrophic events, and that poor communication between the military and local authorities should be corrected by lessons from past disaster missions. Still, some state governors, such as Texas' Rick Perry, cautioned the federal government to "leave decision-making in the hands of local and state leaders and leave for our military the most important job of fighting wars and keeping the peace" (*National Journal's Congress Daily AM* 2005). Other proposals have suggested creating a civilian reserve (or response) corps to assist during disasters and to help rebuild struggling nations (Matthews 2008 and Bennett 2009).

Whether disaster relief is being carried out at home or overseas, however, the reality is that it does not call for an either-or type of approach (such as local versus central government or civilian versus military assets). All of these actors work together in different ways and to varying degrees of intensity depending on the circumstance. No two emergencies will ever be exactly the same, which underscores the value of a high awareness among all the potential responders about each other's cultures and capabilities, as well as the value of developing common procedures for coordination.

In Japan, although the SDF has experience assisting local governments and populations in times of crisis, its relationships with civilian institutions are changing. Civil society in Japan, led by a small number of NGOs, is developing greater capabilities to assist government entities with various services, including disaster relief and consequence management. The need for this role has arisen from decentralization efforts as well as legislative changes aimed at expanding the NGOs' resource base. In recent years, NGO networks in Japan have been formed to improve their ability to work together and to respond to a domestic disaster, though their interaction with the SDF and other countries' NGOs has been quite limited to date.[2] In contrast to its counterparts in the United States, therefore, the SDF has relatively extensive disaster relief training practices and capabilities, but its NGO partners are less well developed and the SDF is still only in the early stages of learning how to integrate a response with NGOs. This situation (almost the opposite of that of the United States) highlights the opportunity for the two countries to learn from each other their various approaches to collaborating overseas or integrating civilian and military responses to domestic disasters.

Japanese NGOs also have little experience working closely with the SDF or other national militaries in international disaster relief situations, but this too is slowly changing as Japanese NGOs strengthen their capabilities and participate more frequently in multilateral operations. Japan has had a legal framework for providing overseas emergency aid since 1987, when the Law Concerning the Dispatch of Japan Disaster Relief Teams (JDR Law) was enacted. In 1992, the JDR Law was revised to enable SDF participation in order to facilitate the dispatch of larger relief teams, to enable teams to conduct operations in disaster areas in a more self-sufficient way, and to upgrade the means of transportation. After experiencing difficulties responding to the humanitarian crisis in Kosovo in 1999, Japanese government officials believed that insufficiently funded Japanese NGOs could not effectively and independently conduct their activities in such an international setting, so they created an institution called Japan Platform. Working closely with the Ministry of Foreign Affairs (MOFA), Japan Platform pre-registers certain Japanese NGOs to receive grants for overseas emergency relief activities and facilitates joint planning, preparation, and logistical support for such missions.

Japanese NGOs generally are not yet sure how to respond when difficult CMCoord questions are raised, though the issue is less controversial

---

2   One example is the Japan Disaster Relief Network (J-Net), established in 2000 under the leadership of the Nippon Volunteer Network Active in Disaster (NVNAD).

for disaster relief operations than it is for humanitarian assistance in conflict areas. Several Japanese NGOs are active in places like Afghanistan and Iraq, for example, where they have refused to accept even small grants from the U.S. military to carry out certain projects, for fear of being too closely identified with the U.S.-led coalition there. In addition, although then-Foreign Minister Kawaguchi Yoriko said that Japan should contribute to Iraqi development on an "all Japan" basis, using the resources of the government, SDF, NGOs, and private corporations, many Japanese NGOs opposed the dispatch of the SDF on the grounds that involvement of the military in development and humanitarian assistance would jeopardize the neutrality of the NGOs' activities (Asia Press Network 2004).

The final report of a security and defense committee appointed by the prime minister in 2004 emphasized the need for "the contribution of personnel and various types of human resources acting in close collaboration with each other, including the SDF, the police, government administrators, Official Development Assistance related organizations, private enterprises, NGOs, and others." The report also urged the Japanese government to "establish guidelines that clearly delineate what is expected of the SDF and what is expected of civilian agents" (Council on Security and Defense Capabilities 2004, 70).

The Japan Association of Corporate Executives study group on Iraqi issues also compiled a report on Japan's future development assistance framework, pointing out the need to clarify roles for the SDF and the private sector in international aid activities. The report concluded that Japan could establish a Japanese equivalent of CMCoord and that as a start the government should promote communication among the SDF, police, coast guard, and civil organizations including international NGOs, because their interface is too limited at the moment (Japan Association of Corporate Executives 2004, 4-7). While serious discussion of the issue of CMCoord is relatively new in Japan, the topic will be increasingly important in domestic and multilateral forums. Moreover, close U.S.-Japan communication during the development of CMCoord will help ensure that "Japanese style" CMCoord does not develop in ways that make it difficult to integrate with other nations.

All of this confirms many of the findings of past IFPA projects on U.S.-Japan-Korea cooperation to manage complex contingencies and on crisis management reforms in the United States and Japan (see Schoff 2005 and 2004). That is, in Japan and the United States (and among America's allies) broad-based interest and support exist for building and strengthening networks and capabilities among the wide range of actors that respond to domestic and international disasters, but communication and mutual understanding regarding their respective approaches, capabilities, and priorities remain insufficient to allow for more than incremental progress. Fortunately, this project and other similar private and government initiatives have begun to bridge these gaps.

Beyond the United States and Japan, the United Nations has, of course, conducted a series of studies and issued guidelines regarding CMCoord in humanitarian crises over the last fifteen or so years. In fact, it was during the 1990s that the current UN system for overseeing and supporting disaster relief missions began to take shape. In December 1991, the General Assembly adopted Resolution 46/182, designed to strengthen the UN's response to both complex emergencies and natural disasters in part by creating a high-level position of emergency relief coordinator (ERC) to centralize control, as well as by establishing the Inter-Agency Standing Committee (IASC), the Consolidated Appeals Process (CAP), and the Central Emergency Revolving Fund (CERF). Soon thereafter and over the course of two years, the UN drafted its *Guidelines on the Use of Military and Civil Defense Assets in Disaster Relief* (also known as the Oslo Guidelines), which established a basic framework for the use of foreign military assets and expertise by relevant international organizations during the disaster relief operations (UN 1994).

As part of the secretary-general's program of reform in 1998, the Department of Humanitarian Affairs was reorganized into the Office for the Coordination of Humanitarian Affairs (OCHA), and its mandate was expanded to include the coordination of humanitarian response and policy development. OCHA was quickly put to the test by hurricane Mitch, and it has been particularly challenged by large-scale disasters in the last few years in South and Central Asia. According to OCHA, "The unprecedented deployment in 2005 of military forces and assets in support of humanitarian response to natural disasters...confirmed the need to update the 1994 Oslo Guidelines," and the new version was released in November 2007 (UN 2007). Other important releases since that time include the *Civil-Military Guidelines and Reference for Complex*

Emergencies in March 2008 (UN 2008a) and the *United Nations Civil-Military Officer Field Handbook* (UN 2008b).

NGOs have also contributed to the CMCoord dialogue throughout this time, either as members of panels developing some of the documents mentioned above, or on their own through training manuals and videos. Several regional organizations and initiatives in Asia have contributed as well, with a particular focus on applying lessons learned from recent disasters and building up regional capacity for prevention and response.

Given the lessons learned from the tsunami relief efforts and many other case studies, it is clear that joint consultation, planning, and exercises between militaries and civilian agents in domestic, bilateral, and multilateral frameworks can greatly enhance the capacity for domestic and international crisis and disaster response. The challenge, however, is how to make this work in a practical manner. It is relatively easy to prescribe additional joint planning, training, workshops, and exercises as a way to improve cooperation in crisis response or disaster relief situations. But the reality is that all the national militaries, government and UN agencies, and NGOs are working with limited staffs and budgets, and they do not always share the same training priorities or political freedom of action. Putting together multilateral exercises is a time-consuming and complicated task, which only gets more difficult as more participants are added to the roster.

The mere fact that improving crisis response coordination is difficult, however, should not dissuade organizations and leaders from pursuing this goal. All the hard work, interaction, and compromise that go into putting together a bilateral or multilateral exercise (that is, what makes it difficult to achieve) are precisely what makes the effort valuable. The overall success of the joint civil-military response to the Indian Ocean tsunami was a direct result of the work that was done before at Cobra Gold (a multilateral civil-military exercise) and many other official and unofficial initiatives. The ability to cooperate effectively does not just materialize. It is planned for and practiced. For multilateral responses, the ideal situation is to work together as a group on a regular basis, but this is often logistically impossible. Strengthening key bilateral relationships, however, is more practical and can go a long way to improving the way that these partners cooperate as members of impromptu coalitions. The U.S.-Japan relationship is particularly important in this regard.

Governments obviously have a key role to play when it comes to developing and strengthening these networks, but CMCoord is a difficult issue for governments to address, since by definition it involves many actors largely beyond their control or influence. Some government initiatives are being undertaken, but much more can be done to enhance these networks and to help identify priorities for common study. IFPA's previous work on crisis management cooperation issues inspired us to design this project in a way that brings together NGO, UN agency, and national and local government leaders across disciplines (for example, specialists in disaster relief, assessment, logistics, contracting, communications, and medicine) to help develop a consensus with regard to cooperation priorities and to stimulate new initiatives and relationships that can enhance the process of cooperation. This approach produced a rich and dynamic bilateral dialogue; this report describes the result of that exchange.

CMCOORD ON THE DOMESTIC STAGE

Domestic CMCoord and international CMCoord share many common characteristics, but they also have distinct qualities. First, many aspects of the military side of the equation are relevant in both domestic and international settings, since any adjustments to unit organization and training will likely be applicable to both domestic and international catastrophes (indeed, if dedicated disaster response capabilities are created within the military, they should be deployable both at home and abroad). Second, for truly large-scale disasters, even the internationally active NGOs often mobilize to contribute domestically, as Mercy Corps did in response to hurricane Katrina or as Japanese NGOs did during a significant earthquake in Niigata in 2004. Finally, there is also an indirect overlap between domestic and international events in terms of incorporating the contributions from other countries, since even wealthy nations can benefit from well-targeted assistance.[3]

Many characteristics of domestic and international operations are clearly dissimilar, however, in important ways. Often, the NGOs and UN agencies that work in the international sphere are not the same agencies that will respond to domestic emergencies (at least when it comes to wealthy countries like Japan and the United States), and they typical-

---

3   Such assistance for disasters in the United States or Japan would likely be limited and called upon only in extreme cases, but examples could include mobile hospitals, temporary housing, water purification systems, or power generators, and they could perhaps be drawn from a ready reserve pre-designated by a handful of wealthy nations.

ly are more numerous than those that involve themselves in domestic disasters. Further, the legal and political circumstances surrounding domestic and international events are usually quite different, and organizations that respond to international crises have the added challenge of operating with multiple languages and cultures. Although U.S.-Japan disaster relief cooperation is likely to be most substantive in the international context, it is still important to understand the domestic foundation on which each country has built its approach to CMCoord, as well as how attitudes and policies are changing.

The United States

The September 11, 2001, terrorist attacks in the United States prompted a major overhaul of federal crisis response plans and policies for responding to catastrophic domestic events, whether resulting from natural occurrences like hurricanes and earthquakes or from terrorist attacks, possibly including the use of WMDs. The U.S. government established the Department of Homeland Security (DHS) at the start of 2003, which quickly began to draft a new national plan for responding to large-scale disasters, working in collaboration with a wide variety of stakeholders and partners around the country. The government's National Response Plan (NRP) was released at the end of 2004, and it continues to be updated (it is now known as the National Response Framework, or NRF).[4] One important goal of the plan was to improve interagency and civil-military coordination during a relief operation by establishing, together with the National Incident Management System (NIMS), "a single, comprehensive framework for management of domestic incidents" (U.S. Department of Homeland Security 2004).

The government's NRP was put to its first big test during hurricane Katrina in the summer of 2005, which was the first time the president designated a catastrophe an "incident of national significance" under

---

4   The National Response Plan was revised and re-released in January 2008 as the National Response Framework (NRF), because earlier versions were deemed to be too bureaucratic and they "did not constitute a true operational plan in the sense understood by emergency managers" (U.S. Department of Homeland Security 2008, 2). More information about the NRF and various annexes can be found at the NRF Resource Center at http://www.fema.gov/emergency/nrf.

the new plan.[5] Although extensive local, state, and federal resources were mobilized to respond, the lack of coordination and timely damage assessments, communication problems, and logistical shortfalls overwhelmed response efforts across all government and non-government levels. The inadequate disaster response to hurricane Katrina demonstrated the limitations of the nation's readiness and ability to react to a major domestic incident, and it renewed discussion about possible ways to enhance such preparations including the possibility of a stronger federal, and perhaps even military, lead role in certain circumstances. The following few pages outline how America responds to large-scale disasters, with a particular focus on lessons learned from Katrina.

Local and state response to disaster relief

As in most countries, emergency response in the United States is managed at the lowest possible jurisdictional level – typically the local government – with the state government becoming involved when local resources (police, fire, public health and medical, emergency management, and other personnel) have been, or are expected to be, overwhelmed. A key partner for state and local governments is the American Red Cross, which responds to thousands of disasters, large and small, every year. Although the Red Cross is not a government agency, it was chartered by the U.S. Congress in 1905 to "carry on a system of national and international relief... [in response to] fire, floods, and other great national calamities." In addition to its support of local authorities for even the smallest of tragedies, such as a house fire, it is also an integral part of the NRF.[6] Today, the Red Cross has an annual budget of over $3.6 billion, and it spends around $500 million on domestic disaster services (American Red Cross 2008).

---

5   The term "incident of national significance" was first coined in the NRP. It refers to events in which federal assistance has been requested by local and state entities for major natural or man-made disasters, or more than one federal agency has become involved in response to imminent or actual acts of terrorism, or the secretary of homeland security has been directed by the president to assume responsibility for managing the response to the disaster.

6   The Red Cross is the only NGO assigned primary agency responsibility for a so-called emergency support function (ESF) under the NRP. It serves as a primary agency, along with the Federal Emergency Management Agency (FEMA), to lead and coordinate federal efforts for ESF 6: Mass Care, Housing, and Human Services.

When state resources are exhausted, state governors may request assistance from neighboring states through the Emergency Management Assistance Compact (EMAC) or directly from the federal government under a presidential disaster or emergency declaration.[7] State governors may also call up members of the National Guard under their control to respond to domestic emergencies, including natural disasters, civil unrest, terrorist incidents, and other complex contingencies.

National Guard troops can be activated by state governors or by the president. The nature of the emergency determines which of these governing authorities calls up the troops and the corresponding duty status under which they serve:

- In a domestic emergency, the state governor can call up the National Guard, and the troops serve under state-active duty status. The operation is commanded by state-level authorities and is funded by the state. Since the National Guard remains under state control at this duty level, it is not subject to the Posse Comitatus Act, which restricts the use of federal military forces within the U.S. homeland, particularly for law enforcement activities.

- In a domestic emergency with homeland security implications, the state governor can, with the approval of the secretary of defense, mobilize the National Guard, and the Guard serves under Title 32 full-time National Guard duty status. The troops remain under state control but the operation receives federal funding to conduct homeland defense activities. Since the state retains control, the forces are not subject to the Posse Comitatus Act.

- In a war or national emergency, the president has the authority, with the consent of the state governors, to call up the National Guard. Troops thus federalized serve under Title 10 active-duty status, and they are considered to be part of the full-time federal military forces and under the command of the president. Under Title 10 status, National Guard troops

---

7   EMAC is a congressionally approved national disaster-relief compact that enables a disaster-affected state to request assistance from other member states. It serves as a legally binding contractual agreement, under which the receiving state is responsible for reimbursing the states that provide assistance.

are directed on the ground by the DoD and operate under the appropriate combatant command. Under Title 10, National Guard troops are subject to Posse Comitatus restrictions.

Confusion surrounding National Guard troop status disrupted the Katrina response effort. Initially, National Guard troops, including those from other states, were called on to assist under state-active duty status. In order to access federal funds in support of Katrina-related disaster relief operations, National Guard personnel were transferred from state-active duty to Title 32 duty. Although the federal government considered transferring National Guard personnel to Title 10 status, officials dismissed this option in order to avoid the political and legal implications of federalizing the National Guard forces, particularly if state governors resisted surrendering control of the National Guard troops under their command or if Title 10 forces were confronted with law-and-order challenges, for which they would face Posse Comitatus Act restrictions. Instead, separate active-duty forces were deployed in support of the Federal Emergency Management Agency (FEMA) and other civil authorities. U.S. Northern Command (NORTHCOM) commanded the federal military response to hurricane Katrina, while the state governors directed the National Guard forces in their states.

The failure to fully integrate active-duty and National Guard forces, however, led to some inefficiencies and duplication of effort. For example, the search and rescue operations of the National Guard, federal military responders, and the Coast Guard were never fully coordinated, resulting in multiple organizations assigning search and rescue tasks without knowing which missions had been completed and which missions still needed to be performed (GAO 2006a, 8). A key challenge is that the National Guard and the active-duty forces plan and train for these missions independently, and they do not have an integrated communications or command structure. This problem was highlighted by a report on the future of the National Guard and reserves, which noted the significant lack of communication between reserve officials and other military leaders, DHS, and NORTHCOM (Commission on the National Guard and Reserves 2007).

Bridging this gap is not easy, as any simple solution requires one side to compromise its authority. As noted earlier, some in Washington think that DoD should take the lead role during a large-scale disaster, but the respected Commission on the National Guard and the Reserves recommended the opposite, that governors be given more command authority over active-duty troops responding to local emergencies (2007). This dilemma of how to integrate active-duty and National Guard forces is mirrored on the international stage, since it is similar to how different national militaries might interact on the scene of a large disaster overseas. They too plan and train separately, and though they are willing to work together, they are reluctant to put themselves under another's control, and often are prohibited from doing so. It will be interesting to see how U.S. defense officials bridge this coordination gap with regard to domestic crises, as it might provide some useful cues for international players.

As one would expect, the Red Cross played a substantial role in the immediate response to hurricane Katrina. This charitable organization distributed financial assistance to over 1.2 million families, provided 3.42 million overnight stays in 1,100 shelters across the country, and served over 52 million meals (U.S. House of Representatives 2006, 343-44). Despite this massive response, the magnitude and severity of the disaster was much larger than the Red Cross was equipped to handle. The Red Cross lacked the logistics capacity to reach affected areas and was dependent on FEMA and DoD for assistance. Although the Red Cross had embedded staff at most relevant state and federal emergency operating centers, the relief agency experienced significant communication and coordination breakdowns with FEMA. Some of the Red Cross's requests for fuel and mobile refrigeration equipment were never processed, and FEMA often failed to coordinate the transportation of evacuees, making it difficult for the Red Cross to track and shelter hurricane victims.

Relevant to this project, several after-action reports regarding Red Cross activity during the Katrina response provide little mention of actual, or even attempted, collaboration with the National Guard or federal forces. This is surprising given that the Red Cross is the official disaster relief entity of the United States, and it assists with a number of so-called emergency support functions (ESFs) that are designated within the NRF. For example, the Red Cross is a primary agency for ESF 6: Mass Care, Housing, and Human Services, and it serves as a supporting agency for ESF 3: Public Works and Engineering, which is led by the U.S. Army Corps of Engineers. Moreover, the Red Cross plays a role in several other ESFs that involve the Defense Department, including emergency management, public health and medical services, agriculture and natural resources, and long-term community recovery and mitigation. Amid the criticisms that have been leveled against the Red Cross for its apparent inability to reach disaster sites quickly, there is clearly a need to facilitate greater cooperation between the Red Cross and the American military, at least in the area of logistical support.[8]

The federal response to disaster relief
Hurricane Katrina was a catastrophe whose scope and destruction severely tested all levels of government. The disaster left more than fifteen hundred dead, affected over ninety thousand square miles, caused at least $80 billion in damage, and displaced an estimated six hundred thousand households from across five states along the Gulf Coast (GAO 2006b, 10). Even before Katrina struck, it was obvious that federal help would be necessary, and so President George W. Bush instructed DHS and DoD in advance to be ready to respond. Despite the mass pooling of local, state, federal, private, and NGO resources, however, the overall response "fell far short of the seamless, coordinated effort that had been envisioned" under the new disaster response architecture adopted in the aftermath of 9/11 (White House 2006, 3).

The National Response Framework describes the federal approach to domestic disaster response for "incidents of national significance," incorporating best practices from a variety of crisis management disciplines, including fire, emergency management, law enforcement, public works, and emergency medical services. The NRF outlines the roles and responsibilities of all local, state, and federal agencies involved in domestic incident management, as well as nongovernmental actors such as nonprofit and volunteer organizations, the private sector, and ordinary citizens. Nothing in the NRF violates the existing authorities or responsibilities of local, state, or federal agencies.

In addition, the NRF identifies fifteen emergency support functions for coordinating national support to local and state entities during inci-

---

8   See, for example, U.S. House of Representatives 2005; Terhune 2005; and New York Times 2005.

dents of national significance.[9] The ESFs range from transportation and communication capabilities to urban search and rescue and emergency management to disaster housing and nutrition assistance, requiring assistance from government agencies as diverse as the departments of Homeland Security, State, Commerce, Labor, Transportation, Agriculture, and Housing and Urban Development. The ESFs can be activated independently of each other, depending on the type of disaster. A large-scale event could trigger activation of all ESFs, while a localized incident such as a tornado might only require the activation of a few ESFs.

As the core operational framework of incident management, the NRF describes national-level coordinating structures and processes that will be employed in conjunction with local and state entities to manage catastrophic events.[10] Overall coordination for federal incident management activities is executed by the secretary of homeland security through multi-agency emergency operating centers at the headquarters, regional, and field levels. Within this coordinating framework, FEMA is no longer the primary agency managing the federal response to domestic disasters (though the FEMA administrator is the principal advisor to the president and the DHS secretary regarding emergency management issues). Instead, all federal departments and agencies involved in disaster response and recovery activities report directly to the secretary of homeland security. The response to hurricane Katrina, however, revealed unresolved issues regarding lines of authority. The lack of clarity, particularly in the field, resulted in disjointed efforts by many federal agencies, a myriad of processes for requesting assistance, and confusion about who should be advised of what requests and what resources would be provided within specific timeframes (GAO 2006a, 20). Subsequent revisions to the NRF have presumably corrected this problem.

---

9   The fifteen ESFs are 1) transportation; 2) communications, 3) public works and engineering; 4) firefighting; 5) emergency management; 6) mass care, housing, and human services; 7) resource support; 8) public health and medical services; 9) urban search and rescue; 10) oil and hazardous materials response; 11) agriculture and natural resources; 12) energy; 13) public safety and security; 14) long-term community recovery and mitigation; and 15) external affairs.

10   The NRF includes a series of annexes that describe ESF, supporting aspects common to all incidents, incident-specific responses for seven broad incident categories, and partner guides.

Briefly described, federal support for disaster relief is coordinated at a joint field office (JFO), which is established locally to provide a central point for federal, state, and local officials to coordinate response and recovery actions. The JFO is headed by the principal federal officer (PFO), who is usually someone designated by the secretary of homeland security (for Katrina, this was the FEMA director, Michael Brown). In theory, the job of the JFO is to facilitate federal support to an established incident command system (ICS), and the ICS is typically handled at the lowest possible jurisdictional level. This can get quite complicated and confusing during large-scale disasters, however, when there is no single and clearly recognized "incident commander." Again, in theory, all of the Defense Department's support is supposed to be coordinated through one person at the JFO, known as the defense coordinating officer (DCO). But as seen after Katrina, the JFO did not function properly in this regard. Two days after the storm hit, the U.S. general leading the military component of the relief effort could not even get in touch

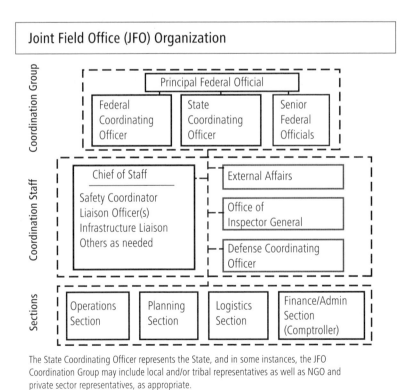

Joint Field Office (JFO) Organization

Coordination Group

Principal Federal Official

Federal Coordinating Officer | State Coordinating Officer | Senior Federal Officials

Coordination Staff

Chief of Staff

Safety Coordinator
Liaison Officer(s)
Infrastructure Liaison
Others as needed

External Affairs

Office of Inspector General

Defense Coordinating Officer

Sections

Operations Section | Planning Section | Logistics Section | Finance/Admin Section (Comptroller)

The State Coordinating Officer represents the State, and in some instances, the JFO Coordination Group may include local and/or tribal representatives as well as NGO and private sector representatives, as appropriate.

with the PFO, and FEMA aides were not sure where to find their director (Hsu 2005).

The DoD's contributions to disaster relief efforts are described as defense support of civil authorities (DSCA), and according to the NRF, requests for DCSA should originate from the JFO. U.S. Northern Command is responsible for DSCA and homeland defense duties. In the case of Katrina, NORTHCOM began its alert and coordination procedures in advance of Katrina's landfall on August 29, 2005; however, many military assets did not reach the affected area until after the presidential declaration of a federal emergency and the declaration of an incident of national significance were made on August 30 and August 31, respectively. After the declarations were made, NORTHCOM sent DCOs to all the potentially affected states, established a joint task force (JTF-Katrina) in support of FEMA relief efforts, and deployed medical personnel, helicopters, ships, and construction battalion engineers. In Louisiana, four MH-53 *Sea Stallion* and two HH-60 *Seahawk* helicopters from USS *Bataan* were flying medical-evacuation and search and rescue missions within days of Katrina's landfall (Miles 2005).

Additional aircraft from the army and air force, including aircraft capable of nighttime search and rescue missions, were transporting FEMA teams to the affected states to assess the damage and gain situational awareness. A wide range of other military members and assets were also called to the area, including the *Iwo Jima* amphibious readiness group, loaded with disaster response equipment, the USNS *Comfort*, a hospital ship equipped with medical personnel and supplies, and USS *Grapple*, a Navy rescue and salvage vessel prepared to support maritime and underwater survey and salvage operations (Miles 2005). However, most of these assets, as well as additional active-duty forces, did not arrive until September 5, seven days after hurricane Katrina hit. It should be noted, however, that naval assets are generally not prepared to respond immediately to a quick-hitting disaster, given the required transit time.

Several factors influenced DoD's incremental response to the situation. First, although the Pentagon began deploying personnel and resources before the storm made landfall, it could not fully respond until the presidential declaration of a federal emergency and declaration of an incident of national significance were issued, and in response to DHS and FEMA formal requests for military support. The formal requests did not come until four days after Katrina struck. Second, both the NRP and the DoD's Strategy for Homeland Defense and Civil Support (released in June 2005) promote the National Guard as the primary military response in support of civil authorities. Although both documents recognize that active-duty forces can also play a critical role depending on the nature of the event, the guiding principle is that DoD is a supporting agency and a resource of last resort, particularly in response to natural disasters. During the Katrina response, DoD initially relied on the National Guard to respond, but growing concerns about the severity of the disaster prompted DoD to supplement National Guard troops with active-duty personnel. However, neither document specified either how DoD resources should be used to support federal agencies or what resources it should provide in the event of a domestic disaster.

Third, the DoD plan for providing military assistance to civil authorities (U.S. Department of Defense 1993), which was undergoing revision at the time of the Katrina crisis, also neglected to address key questions of integration, command and control, timeframes for response, and the division of tasks between National Guard resources under state control and federal resources under NORTHCOM (GAO 2006a, 10). As a result, critical military assets were not utilized, such as communications equipment and reconnaissance and surveillance assets, all of which would have provided additional situational awareness and improved communication between responders. Finally, the failure to fully integrate and coordinate the National Guard, active-duty units, and other state and federal responders led to several inefficiencies, including a lack of clarity in search and rescue missions and poor visibility of logistics requirements. Finally, the DoD often made its own damage assessments and began deploying its resources without knowing the full extent of the damage or the required assistance (GAO 2006a, 7).

Despite these challenges, the military mounted an impressive response, which in the end included over twenty-two thousand active-duty personnel and fifty thousand National Guard troops, more than 80 airplanes, 50 ships, and 360 helicopters (U.S. Northern Command 2005a and 2005b). Indeed, after the White House reported in its assessment of the federal response to hurricane Katrina that the military, National Guard, and Coast Guard were the only entities that proved truly effective during the response to that event, revisions to the NRF have been undertaken to redefine the military role in domestic disaster management. Plans to designate DoD as the lead federal agency for certain large-scale disasters have also been discussed.[11] State governors are resisting such efforts, however, fearing that the changes would enable the president to federalize the National Guard during a domestic incident without the consent of the state governors. Nevertheless, DoD has announced plans to embed defense officials into FEMA regional offices, fold support from federal reconnaissance agencies into the military's civil support processes, and conduct exercises to improve interagency planning and coordination.

Interagency coordination is a particularly tough challenge for the government and the military, and U.S. efforts to address this issue may contain useful lessons for Japan, which has begun to make significant structural changes in the last few years to the SDF, the Ministry of Defense (MOD), MOFA, and the Cabinet Secretariat that severely test the government's and the military's ability to coordinate effectively during stressful events. In the United States, NORTHCOM, as well as every combatant command, has a joint interagency coordination group (JIACG) already in place to facilitate interagency relationships, with representatives from the federal government, the National Guard, the Coast Guard, other combatant commands, academia, the private sector, nongovernmental organizations, and law enforcement, as well as partners from Canada and Mexico. The emergency preparedness and planning division of the interagency coordination directorate focuses on DSCA operations and on those agencies and operations associated with natural and man-made incidents. JIACG has working groups on issues of special interest, such as natural disaster, pandemic influenza, private-sector engagement, and scripted mission assignments.

Despite these efforts, however, several Katrina after-action assessments characterized the coordination between the Defense Department and DHS, and FEMA in particular, as ineffective. One report recommended that NORTHCOM better integrate with FEMA and the National Guard because a lack of effective information-sharing mechanisms impeded more efficient civil-military coordination during the Katrina response (U.S. House of Representatives 2006, 201). To prevent such

---

11 For a discussion of the role of the military in disaster relief, see Business Roundtable 2006.

failures in the future, NORTHCOM and the National Guard Bureau have purchased deployable communications systems and interoperable communications equipment (Fein 2006).

Overall, improving civil-military coordination also depends on forward-looking assessments of what resources are needed and when those resources will be needed, as well as an understanding of the roles and responsibilities of each agency involved in the disaster response. To this end, JIACG is developing scripted requests for assistance (RFAs) based on certain scenarios that anticipate requests for federal and military support, as well as identifying the strengths and weaknesses of each agency involved in a relief effort. If scripted RFAs can strike the right balance between specificity and flexibility, they could be a great asset to disaster managers at all levels. Some involved in these efforts hope that such planning and preparation activities can even go beyond generic RFAs and begin to address the implications of certain policies in the context of specific scenarios: disaster management planners cannot anticipate every problem, but efforts should be made to plan for as many as possible. As an example, one U.S. official noted at a 2006 workshop, "During the Katrina response, road blocks were set up to prevent sightseers from wandering into dangerous areas, but those same road blocks turned away transport trucks loaded with relief supplies" (IFPA-OSIPP 2006).

Private-sector response to disaster relief
An interesting feature of recent disaster planning and response efforts has been the increased role for, and contributions from, private corporations. This has become evident not only in terms of financial donations, but also in the companies' willingness and ability to provide operational support across several functional areas, including strategy development, logistics, and communications.[12] For all of the benefits that this vast pool of capabilities and resources brings, however, the private sector presents another coordination challenge to local and federal responders, despite corporations' apparent enthusiasm to contribute during times of crisis.

During hurricane Katrina, for example, Anheuser Busch donated 9.4 million cans of safe drinking water to victims, and it was able to le-

---

12   For more detail on these and other private-sector contributions to the hurricane Katrina response effort, see Business Civic Leadership Center 2005.

verage its packaging operations, logistics personnel, and government affairs office to distribute the supplies. Ford Motor Company sent 275 vans, pickup trucks, and sport-utility vehicles to law enforcement personnel in the disaster region and dispatched a mobile command center to serve as a temporary headquarters for a local sheriff's office in Louisiana that had been destroyed. Wal-Mart's efforts began even before the storm made landfall, as its emergency operations center pre-positioned relief supplies and response teams around the Gulf Coast. Interestingly, the company's relief inventory was developed through trend analyses that revealed what communities usually need to purchase before, during, and after a disaster. The Home Depot also began mobilizing four days before hurricane Katrina blasted the Gulf Coast, stocking stores with electricity generators and rebuilding supplies. In fact, the company's rapid response was a result of planning efforts, which included reorganizing its regional inventories to match the disasters they confront: earthquakes and wildfires in the West, blizzards in the North, and hurricanes in the South (Fox 2005).

In some cases, private corporations can offer to civilian emergency responders certain capabilities similar to those provided by the military, such as satellite communication links and air and ground transportation. Moreover, businesses are relatively unburdened by chain-of-command and other bureaucratic and legal hurdles that often constrain military engagement. This prompts questions that will need to be addressed going forward, such as, in what circumstances can and should the private sector, rather than the military, assist civilian disaster-response efforts? How can private corporations and the military work together to provide logistical support? Should there be a private-sector- and/or NGO-coordinating component embedded within the JFO structure?

Efforts toward integrating all of these entities are currently underway, such as with the Strong Angel III exercise held in California in August 2006, which conducted an integrated response to a simulated, rapidly spreading, highly-contagious virus. Public-private disaster response cooperation regarding communications and information sharing was the key dynamic being highlighted in this event, and sponsors included the Office of the Secretary of Defense, the Naval Postgraduate School,

Microsoft, Cisco Systems, Sprint Nextel, and Google.[13] The rising importance of the private sector in this realm has also been reflected in the efforts of many organizations to raise awareness of the issue and to help improve the ability of private corporations to contribute in a disaster. These include, among others, the Partnership for Disaster Response of the Business Roundtable, the Disaster Resource Network, and the Business Civic Leadership Council at the U.S. Chamber of Commerce.

Beyond private-sector companies and the Red Cross, the efforts of countless charitable organizations and private donors in the aftermath of hurricane Katrina constituted the largest relief effort in U.S. history, totaling over $3.13 billion in cash and in-kind gifts (U.S. House of Representatives 2006, 343). Disaster relief agencies responding to Katrina assisted with evacuations and the delivery of critical commodities such as food, water, and shelter; provided medical and social services; conducted animal search and rescue missions; and removed debris. Moreover, charities worked together to coordinate the delivery of supplies and shared information through daily conference calls and electronic databases. The National Voluntary Organizations Active in Disaster (NVOAD), a consortium of over thirty recognized national disaster relief organizations, released a relief and recovery assistance guide one month after hurricane Katrina hit, identifying the resources and contact information of federal and relief agencies assisting hurricane victims. The guide included information on a variety of topics, including debris removal, housing, employment and training, funeral arrangements, health and safety, legal assistance, family and pet reunification, and financial assistance.

Everyone involved in disaster management in the United States recognizes that improvements are needed across the spectrum of local, state, federal, and non-governmental entities involved in responding to catastrophic events, particularly in the areas of joint planning, communications, and coordination. It would seem reasonable, for example, to pursue greater planning and training interaction between the National Guard/DoD and the Red Cross and other humanitarian NGOs. After all, one of the core missions of the Red Cross, according to its congressional charter, is to be a "medium of communication between the people of the United States of America and their armies." Yet, official

---

13   For a complete list of participating organizations of the Strong Angel III exercise, see http://www.strongangel3.net.

Red Cross representation in the JFO organization noted above is strikingly absent.

It is reasonable to expect that over the next few years, the United States will be in a better position to provide relatively quick and effective relief to victims of large-scale disasters. A major reason for this will be the focused efforts to improve integration of capabilities that reside in different departments, agencies, and organizations at the national and local levels. Many have likened this effort to the process of integrating the U.S. military service branches to improve their ability to conduct joint operations.[14] The U.S. military has made great strides toward achieving the ultimate objective of this effort, known as jointness, though it is truly a never ending process of communication, interaction, and practice. There is always room to improve, because the different cultures of these organizations, their different vocabulary and procedures, and their institutional pride will often complicate joint planning and operations. This will certainly be the case in the area of disaster relief.

Japan

In most ways, the United States and Japan are a study in contrasts rather than similarities when it comes to their geography and national composition, and many of these differences affect the way that each country responds to large-scale domestic disasters. In contrast to the United States, for example, Japan is geographically small and densely populated. Japan's population, roughly half the size of America's, squeezes into an area about the size of California, and the country's mountainous terrain makes for an even higher degree of population density. Demographically Japan is an older nation (posing unique disaster relief challenges), with one-fifth of its population over sixty-five years of age. This compares to slightly more than one-tenth of the population in the U.S. case. Japan's

---

14   The Goldwater-Nichols Department of Defense Reorganization Act of 1986 (Goldwater-Nichols Act) reworked the command structure of the U.S. military, integrating the branch services (army, air force, navy, and marine corps) under the operational authority of functional (transportation, space, special operations, etc.) and regional (Europe, Pacific, etc.) combatant commanders. The act also designated the chairman of the Joint Chiefs of Staff, as opposed to the service chiefs, as the principal military advisor to the president of the United States, National Security Council, and secretary of defense.

Cabinet Office has warned that demographic and population density trends raise a concern that "Japan's disaster prevention capability may be declining" (Yamaguchi 2007). Its report noted that the number of skyscrapers exceeding the height of one hundred meters has more than quadrupled in the last fifteen years.

Emergency services are also highly centralized in Japan, meaning that there is a national administrative and policy-making umbrella for local police and fire department personnel (the National Police Agency, or NPA, and the Fire and Disaster Management Agency, or FDMA). Although Japan's forty-seven prefecture governments do not have their own national guard units to call upon in times of crisis, they can request support from the nation's self-defense forces. Japan's SDF has averaged more than eight hundred domestic disaster relief operations annually over the last five years, demonstrating how often it assists local responders with emergency patient transportation, search and rescue operations, and firefighting activities (Ministry of Defense of Japan 2008, 187).

The SDF's relatively high tempo of relief operations also underscores how often Japan endures natural disasters, particularly earthquakes and typhoons. Japan experiences a large percentage of the world's earthquakes with a magnitude over 6.5 on the Richter scale (or M6.5), totaling fourteen in 2004 and thirteen in 2005 (or about 15 percent of the world's total). In October 2004, the Niigata Chuetsu earthquake of about M6.8 killed forty-six people and destroyed 2,827 homes. Ten people were killed and more than one thousand made homeless in Niigata by a similar-sized earthquake in 2007, and another ten people died in Miyagi prefecture in a 2008 earthquake.

Of course, the most devastating earthquake since the 1920s occurred in the Kobe-Awaji region in January 1995, killing over sixty-four hundred and destroying more than one hundred thousand homes. Volcanic eruptions in populated areas also occur from time to time, as do extremely heavy snowfalls in some regions. In December 2005 and January 2006, for example, three to four meters of snow fell in Nagano and Niigata prefectures, claiming at least eighty lives, injuring nearly two thousand, isolating numerous villages, and cutting power to over a million households. Japan's high population density also raises the human and economic stakes for industrial accidents, chemical fires, and accidents at nuclear power facilities.

Despite Japan's familiarity with natural disasters, its centralized governing structure, and its wealthy economy, the government demonstrated several crisis management shortcomings in the 1990s that led to substantial reforms.[15] The irony was that, although political, administrative, and budgetary power was concentrated in Tokyo, each ministry and agency controlled its own piece of the crisis management puzzle, and the prime minister had little statutory authority to compel a unified approach to planning, procurement, training, and communication. The most significant reforms, therefore, were designed to enhance the authority of the prime minister to lead and coordinate the various ministries and independent agencies in the Japanese government during a crisis. Other legal changes allow for quicker mobilization and dispatch of the SDF during a disaster, even allowing for direct requests by a town mayor to the SDF or an MOD representative under certain circumstances.[16]

Overshadowing these recent and ongoing reforms is the expectation that a major earthquake will someday strike the Tokyo region, as happened in 1923 when over 140,000 people died. The Japanese Cabinet Office has estimated that as many as 13,000 could be killed in a major modern-day earthquake around Tokyo, while other estimates run as high as 30,000 to 60,000 (Eldridge 2006). Research indicates that the probability of an M8 earthquake in areas near and west of Tokyo within the next thirty years ranges from 50 percent to 87 percent depending on the exact location. This reality sharpens the focus of Japan's disaster relief and prevention specialists. Japan's Central Disaster Prevention Council warned in 2007 that up to 42,000 people could be killed in the Osaka and Kobe area if a large earthquake of M7.6 struck western Japan (Watanabe 2007).

Japan's basic approach to disaster management coordination
As in the United States, Japan delegates responsibility for disaster relief management to the lowest possible jurisdictional level. Given the national affiliation of local fire and police personnel, however, coupled with the de facto national guard role that Japan's SDF plays, the central gov-

---

15   See Schoff 2004 for a case study analysis of the 1995 Kobe earthquake and the
       1999 Tokaimura nuclear accident, as well as for a description of the reforms that
       followed.

16   This refers to a 1995 amendment of the Disaster Countermeasures Basic Act, Article 68-2 (request to call up SDF for disaster relief).

ernment is quite frequently involved in local disaster relief and recovery efforts. The foundation for Japan's disaster management system is the Central Disaster Management Council, placed under the aegis of the Cabinet Office in 2001. The council is chaired by the prime minister and it includes all cabinet ministers (notably the minister of state for disaster management), along with the heads of four designated public corporations (Bank of Japan, Japanese Red Cross Society, Japan Broadcasting Corporation, and Nippon Telegraph and Telephone Corporation) and four academic or technical experts. The council prepares the nation's Basic Disaster Management Plan (Basic Plan), upon which the responsible agencies, organizations, and local governments develop their operation-

The Central Disaster Management Council

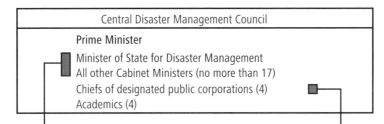

Central Disaster Management Council

Prime Minister
Minister of State for Disaster Management
All other Cabinet Ministers (no more than 17)
Chiefs of designated public corporations (4)
Academics (4)

Secretarial Committee
Parliamentary Secretary of the Cabinet Office
Deputy Chief Cabinet Secretary for Crisis Management
Director-General for Disaster Management, Cabinet Office
Deputy Manager of the Fire and Disaster Management Agency
Directors general from individual ministries

Special Boards of Inquiry
• Special board of inquiry on the Tonankai and Nankai Earthquakes (formed 10/3/2001)
• Special board of inquiry on inheriting the lessons of past disasters (formed 7/31/2003)
• Special board of inquiry on trench-centered earthquakes around the Japan trench and Chisima trench (formed 8/27/2005)
• Special board of inquiry on promoting a national campaign to alleviate damage from disasters (formed 12/9/2005)

Functions
Prepares and promotes implementation of the Basic Disaster Management Plan and the Earthquake Disaster Management Plan.
Prepares and promotes implementation of plans for emergency measures to be implemented in case of disaster.
Deliberates on key matters relating to disaster management in response to referrals from the Prime Minster and/or the Minister of State for Disaster Management (e.g., basic disaster management policies, overall coordination of disaster response measures, declarations of emergency).
Submits views on key matters relating to disaster management to the Prime Minister and the Minister of State for Disaster Management.

al plans. The Basic Plan was almost entirely revised after the 1995 Kobe earthquake, and various components of it have been further revised based on lessons learned in the past decade.

Key players at the national level besides the prime minister include the minister of state for disaster management, the deputy chief cabinet secretary for crisis management, the director general for disaster management in the Cabinet Office, and the NPA commissioner, all of whom report within the immediate cabinet structure (that is, the Cabinet Secretariat and the Cabinet Office). Other critical agencies outside of the Cabinet Secretariat/Cabinet Office framework are the FDMA (officially a part of the Ministry of Internal Affairs and Communications), the Maritime Safety Agency (the Japan Coast Guard, which is part of the Ministry of Land, Infrastructure and Transport), and the Ministry of Defense. All of these key players, together with personnel from other ministries with skills or responsibilities relevant to the particular disaster at hand, can be assembled at a crisis management headquarters specially established at the prime minister's residence depending on the severity of the disaster. There are also cases when the government will establish an on-site disaster management headquarters by dispatching a governmental investigation team to the stricken area, not unlike the JFO in the United States.

The other important components in all this, of course, are the prefectural and local governments and their emergency management teams, since they constitute the first wave of response to a disaster. At the prefecture and municipal levels, there are disaster prevention councils made up from local government agencies, police departments, fire departments, and designated public institutions. These councils are responsible for implementing disaster-reduction programs and overseeing the development of local operational plans. When a significant disaster strikes, the municipal government will create a headquarters for disaster countermeasures (HDC) to manage the local response. An HDC can also be established at the prefecture level if the situation requires a more robust relief effort. Requests for central government assistance generally come from the governor of the prefecture on behalf of town leaders, but under particularly urgent circumstances the mayors can directly request national assistance including from the SDF.

Communication and coordination among all of these key players have improved drastically over the last decade, though the system is still far from perfect. A key challenge continues to be the integration of command and control functions when multiple towns and prefectures are involved. Although prefectures in Japan are analogous to American states in terms of financial clout and political stature, in terms of geographical area they are often more comparable to counties within many U.S. states. This means that a large earthquake or typhoon can quickly affect many prefectures and lead to the establishment of multiple HDCs at the prefecture level. Japan does not have a standardized ICS or a unified command approach for dealing with multiple jurisdictions. Instead, the government tends to rely on parallel disaster management structures that are severely tested during large-scale or rapidly unfolding crises.

Other shortcomings and subsequent lessons learned from past events include insufficient knowledge of the plans and capabilities of other agencies and levels of government, a lack of adequately staffed organizations with responsibility to handle disasters, and a lack of drills or exercises that simulate decision making and test systems to the breaking point. Japanese authorities have been working to address all of these issues, in part by increasing the frequency and substance of national-local collaboration for disaster planning and management, investing in compatible emergency communications systems and a new satellite-based tsunami alert system, and creating more realistic training exercises that do not reveal beforehand the scenarios to which participants will be responding.[17] There have also been efforts to train and deploy more emergency medical technicians (EMTs) among the first responders, who were relatively few in number in the 1990s.

As with many other aspects of disaster management in Japan, the relationship between the central and local governments has been steadily changing in recent years. Local governments have long been assigned a wide range of substantive responsibilities, collectively spending much

---

17 The new satellite alert system is called J-ALERT and was launched on February 9, 2007. J-ALERT can instantly send warnings of tsunamis and updates on volcanic activity to help speed evacuations. The FDMA manages the system, which was first tested in ten prefectures and four cities. The system is relatively expensive, and so the adoption rate by local governments has been lower than originally expected.

more than the central government does on administrative and social services, including disaster prevention and management activities. This is despite the fact that the local governments' tax revenues are about half those of the central government's general account, which results in large financial transfers from the central government in the form of local allocation tax grants and other treasury disbursements (Ministry of Internal Affairs and Communication 2008, chapter 4). Traditionally, this gave central government bureaucracies a lot of regulatory control over local authorities, and local officials were often quite satisfied to accept the money and follow the rules regarding how it should be spent.[18] Since the Kobe earthquake and for other reasons, however, critics have begun to question just how much local capacity this deferential approach was actually building within the communities. Some feared that towns simply became more adept at political and bureaucratic maneuvering to obtain the funds than they were at integrated disaster management with neighboring villages.

Against this backdrop, the central government has been trying to strengthen the administrative foundation of municipalities as part of a decentralization campaign in the past few years, and toward this end it created a number of legal and financial incentives to promote the merger of municipalities. Recent results have been quite dramatic, once the groundwork was laid in the late 1990s and early 2000s. As of July 2008, within Japan's forty-seven prefectures there were 1,787 municipalities plus the twenty-three wards of Tokyo. That compares to about 3,100 municipalities in 2004, or a drop of over 40 percent in just four years, and it represents a remarkable consolidation of disaster prevention, public safety, and disaster management resources (Ministry of Internal Affairs and Communication 2008, chapter 17). The motivations behind this decentralization and consolidation policy are by no means solely tied to improving local disaster response capabilities, but this is certainly one result of a broader trend of divesting more responsibility and accountability to local governments.

---

18   Revenue transfers from the central government to the local governments are also a form of income redistribution, where some local governments with a solid tax base receive no grants at all, while others receive a large proportion of their local revenue from such transfers.

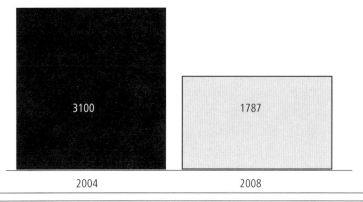

Recent Consolidation of Municipalities in Japan

3100 — 2004

1787 — 2008

Other components of this strategy include more frequent joint emergency training exercises involving the central government and (at times) multiple prefectural governments, and MOD has also made efforts to place former SDF officers in local government positions to bolster the localities' crisis management capabilities. In 2002 there were roughly 25 such SDF officers working in local governments, and by the middle of 2008 there were 150 retired SDF officials serving as staff responsible for disaster prevention in forty-three prefectures and eighty-two cities and towns (Ministry of Defense of Japan 2008, 450).

Apart from the expectation in Japan of a massive earthquake, the trend toward closer central-local government coordination for contingency planning and preparedness is also being driven by regional security concerns and potential threats associated with Japan's support of the United States in the ongoing battle against global terrorist networks. The overall coincidence of the September 11, 2001, terrorist attacks in the United States (and follow-on attacks in places like Bali in 2002, Madrid in 2004, and London in 2005) with North Korea's resumption of its missile and nuclear weapons programs in 2002 and 2003 prompted the Japanese government to consider more seriously the possibility that it could one day be the target of a terrorist or missile attack. This also created a political climate in which policy makers could pass national emergency legislation that began to clarify two key issues long in need of attention: 1) the role of central authorities vis-à-vis local officials in such an emergency and 2) the role of the military in a crisis and consequence management situation. As a result, three new laws were adopted in 2003 that prescribed the basic principles for response to an armed attack (or "anticipated attack"), the respective responsibilities of the national and local governments, and some of the extra-ordinary rights accorded to the SDF during such an emergency in order to respond more effectively.

These new laws only created the basic framework for this kind of emergency response, however, so further deliberation and details were required. Over the next year, bureaucrats and politicians hammered out a set of seven additional bills that clarified a variety of related issues such as the government's and SDF's ability to commandeer land and houses, remove vehicles to clear roads, and draft private organizations to assist with transportation or public communication efforts. Even though these laws were primarily designed to deal with attack scenarios, amendments were made to allow the government to take such measures in "similar emergency cases," meaning that Japan was essentially creating a new legal framework to respond to any kind of large-scale domestic disaster (natural or man-made) (Chikara and Yuichi 2004). The laws also clarified how U.S. Forces in Japan (USFJ) can cooperate with the SDF in these situations, including the mutual provision of supplies and services during disaster relief operations. Basing its work on the new emergency legislation passed in 2003 and 2004, the central government took another nine months to finalize the implementing guidelines for the new laws, which were finally approved by the cabinet in March 2005.

This activity has helped create a closer working relationship between the central and local governments in general, and between the prefectures and the SDF in particular. The laws mentioned above, for example, required local governments to develop civil protection plans to explain how they will manage and assist with evacuations, temporary housing, food, and medical care in the event of an attack. The prefectures and towns had already considered all of these issues to some degree, but they had never done so in such a military context or in such close coordination with the SDF. Some prefectures moved aggressively to establish their civil protection procedures, notably Tottori prefecture by the Sea of Japan and Fukui prefecture, which is home to fifteen nuclear reactors. Follow-up joint exercises have since been carried out annually involving anywhere from five hundred to two thousand central and local government officials (including the SDF) and up to four prefectures in one exercise (Japan Defense Agency 2006, 203, and Chikara and Yuichi 2006). The frequency of these exercises has also increased, as the number of participating prefectures tripled from FY2005 to FY2007 (Ministry of Defense of Japan 2008, 161).

The SDF has also made adjustments to improve its coordination with local governments, in part by establishing the joint Provincial Liaison and Coordination Division in Tokyo and creating the new post of civil protection and disaster relief coordinator in each of the local provincial cooperation headquarters. Whereas for many decades the central and local governments sought to downplay the SDF's involvement, it was perhaps a sign of the SDF's improved reputation when the provincial cooperation headquarters name was officially changed to the SDF Prefectural Cooperation Headquarters, starting in FY 2006. The SDF and prefecture governments use these offices and personnel to identify potential staging areas and communications centers for the SDF in case of a disaster, implementing a numbering system on the roofs of buildings to facilitate identification from the air, and harmonizing response manuals.

A growing role for the SDF and civil society

The SDF's role in domestic and international crisis management contingencies is growing and still evolving. Even though the SDF has long contributed to consequence management operations in Japan, more often than not the nature of its contribution has been a secondary support role, usually focused on recovery activities such as debris removal and the longer-term care and feeding of the affected population. After all, the SDF personnel are not meant to be first responders, and their base of operations is almost always farther from the disaster site than that of the local fire and police personnel. It was only in 1995 that disaster relief support activities were first designated as one of the three roles for the SDF's defense capabilities (Ministry of Foreign Affairs of Japan 1995). A little more than a decade later, international peace cooperation activities were elevated to be a "primary mission" of the SDF (Ministry of Defense of Japan 2008, 114).

As a largely self-sufficient organization, the SDF often takes a day or two to mobilize, and it does not have the kind of daily contact with the local population that local responders do. In addition, the police department keeps detailed and updated records about the local population (who lives where, their ages, even information about physical disabilities or special medical conditions), which helps tremendously during the immediate response. During the Kobe earthquake relief effort, for example, police officers and firefighters were responsible for over 95 percent of live rescues from collapsed buildings. In contrast, the SDF played a more significant role in the recovery of the victims who had not survived the tragedy, demolishing collapsed houses, transporting debris, and assisting with medical treatment or food delivery.

Since the Kobe earthquake, however, and thanks in part to some of the legal and organizational changes described above, awareness among local political leaders about what the SDF can contribute has grown in Japan, and the SDF is able to deploy more quickly than it could before. Local governments have come to appreciate the value of the SDF, which is relatively self-sufficient, provides unique resources under a unity of command, and is accustomed to risky work. Moreover, as local budgets tightened throughout the late 1990s, local authorities also appreciated the fact that they did not need to reimburse the central government for the cost of an SDF dispatch. As voters became more aware of the SDF's capabilities and understood that it was now easier for local officials to request SDF assistance, there was also a political price to pay if the public perceived that a mayor or governor waited too long to seek SDF support. When in doubt, therefore, the default has largely shifted in Japan to a quicker involvement of the SDF as opposed to waiting to see if its services are really necessary.

This phenomenon was clearly evident during the response to the Niigata-Chuestsu earthquake, which struck a mountainous part of central Japan on October 23, 2004, killing sixty-seven people and injuring over four thousand. The rugged terrain complicated access and gave the SDF's helicopters a prominent role in the relief effort. Unlike the situation in Kobe, the SDF was involved in about 35 percent of successful rescues (instead of less than 5 percent), and its troops constituted close to half of the 270,000 relief personnel dispatched to the disaster area. According to one Ground SDF officer, "The most effective thing we did was to decide the action swiftly without waiting for the official order from the prefecture, to obtain the communication method and to grasp the real-time information properly" (Nagamatsu 2006). The SDF also carried out its more traditional role of construction equipment transportation, debris removal, and the provision of food, water, shelter, and bathing facilities. It is also worth noting that the entire rescue effort was covered extensively on television and watched throughout the country, conveying the impression that the SDF is essentially an equal partner to police officers and firefighters when it comes to disaster relief operations.

The Niigata-Chuestu earthquake was a watershed event for more than just the SDF, however, as it signaled the rise of another set of disaster relief players on the scene, namely Japan's internationally active NGOs. Two of Japan's larger indigenous NGOs that have contributed to relief and recovery work around the world (for example, in Iraq, Afghanistan, Lebanon, Sudan, Bosnia, and Sri Lanka) for the first time responded domestically when the earthquake hit in October 2004. Peace Winds Japan (PWJ) dispatched a relief team on the night of the earthquake, equipped with satellite phones, power generators, and emergency shelter units. PWJ's sixteen-day operation included the provision of shelter, medical, and engineering services. Another large Japanese NGO, known as JEN, sent its first domestic relief and recovery team to two particularly hard-hit towns in the region, carrying out relief activities and staying until the end of December to help with rubbish removal, relocation, and emotional support programs. The participation of NGOs like PWJ and JEN in the Niigata relief effort demonstrates a more holistic approach to disaster management in Japan, but it also complicates the central government's drive to streamline decision making and exercise greater control over relief operations. These challenges can certainly be overcome, as long as enough attention and resources are dedicated to preparation and communication.

For over one hundred years the Japanese Red Cross Society (JRCS) had a de facto monopoly on well-organized, nongovernmental assistance in times of a domestic disaster. Today the JRCS still leads the way with 470 volunteer disaster response teams throughout the country (about six thousand members), and it supervises a nation-wide storage and distribution system for food and other materials needed by victims of disasters. By law, the JRCS is required to help coordinate relief activities and to cooperate with the government and other public agencies during relief operations. The JRCS response to the Niigata earthquake, for example, dwarfed that of PWJ or JEN, with almost one thousand volunteers who assisted with the provision of food, clothing, shelter, and necessities. Within one week of the disaster, over $67 million was donated to the victims through JRCS.

The Japanese Red Cross is still the largest disaster relief NGO in Japan, but it is learning to share some of these responsibilities with numerous new domestic players, as well as with the SDF. Given its experience with natural calamities, Japan has always had a fairly high rate of citizen involvement with local disaster management organizations. These issues have long been a part of school curricula, and there is a day set aside nationally each year for schools and towns to conduct training and emergency drills.[19] At the time of the Kobe earthquake, for example, about 45 percent of Japanese households participated in an estimated sixty-five thousand local voluntary disaster management organizations. But this number continues to grow, reaching about 58 percent of households and nearly one hundred thousand organizations by 2001 (Cabinet Office 2002).

The extent to which these groups can contribute constructively during a large-scale disaster, however, is questionable, and in some cases they have perhaps caused more problems than they helped to solve. After the Niigata earthquake, for example, the municipal government of Nagaoka changed its policies and decided not to accept relief goods from the public if another large disaster strikes. Thousands of tiny disaster relief organizations donated goods with the best of intentions, but the generosity required an excessive amount of time to sort and distribute the items, and some clothes remained in storage up to a year after the disaster, leading to additional costs for the local government. As a result of the new policy, the city of Nagaoka will only accept relief goods from other local governments, companies, and organizations with which it has special agreements in place (*Daily Yomiuri* 2006a).

In contrast, another town in Japan has gone out of its way to recruit new volunteers to assist in times of crisis, and it is focused particularly on citizens over sixty years old. In this case, the city of Takarazuka (near Osaka) is approaching soon-to-retire municipal government workers with experience in disaster relief and recovery from the Kobe earthquake, in

---

19   Disaster Management Day in Japan falls on September 1 each year, and it commemorates the devastating Great Kanto Earthquake of 1923, which killed over 140,000 people.

an effort to preserve that institutional knowledge (*Daily Yomiuri* 2006b). In this way, the city is proactively targeting volunteers with specific skills and channeling their contributions in the area of planning, preparations, and neighborhood relations. As time goes on, Japan will need to continue in this direction of professionalizing and streamlining NGO participation in disaster relief operations, since it remains in the very early stages of integrating nongovernmental assistance into its still-evolving national disaster management architecture.

It is important to remember that Japan's NGO community is not as mature or well funded as its counterpart in the United States. Legal and financial hurdles to establishing substantial nonprofit organizations in Japan have kept their numbers relatively low, and contributors to these organizations are not eligible for the same tax deductions that Americans receive, which obviously makes fundraising a challenge. This, in turn, has limited employment opportunities, and in Japan's rigid labor market it has been difficult for NGOs to attract and retain a professional workforce. All of this is gradually changing, as Japanese NGOs work to improve their financial and technical strength, but this will take time. Japanese NGOs do have some outstanding leaders and staff members, but not yet enough of them to meet the needs.

The traditional government-NGO relationship in Japan is also different from that in the United States. For many years in Japan, most noteworthy nonprofit organizations had some formal affiliation with a government ministry, and even if the connection was institutionally weak, the nonprofits still required official certification from the "competent ministry," which pretty much ensured that only groups with missions consistent with the relevant ministry's policies would be certified. At that point, the certified nonprofits would be eligible for grants from the ministry (or maybe to hire newly retired ministry bureaucrats), which further tied the organizations' future to ministry approval. In fact, because of the relatively small number of truly independent NGOs, the common way to refer to these groups was nonprofit organizations (NPOs) so as not to mislead people into thinking there were no government strings attached.[20]

---

20 For the sake of simplicity in this report, NPOs and NGOs are generally referred to collectively as NGOs, unless a special distinction is necessary.

During the 1960s, 1970s, and 1980s in Japan, most high-profile independent NGOs were usually small local groups vehemently opposed to some government initiative such as the Narita airport expansion, the building of a local dam, or the hosting of U.S. military forces. Even though the situation is different today, and many more indigenous NGOs and NPOs are involved in education, health care, disaster management, and other sectors of the civil society, the lingering impression among a good number of senior-level bureaucrats is that NGOs are predisposed to be anti-establishment or that they cannot be sufficiently professional and accountable. These attitudes can retard the growth of productive government-NGO partnerships in Japan.

One way to streamline NGO and NPO interaction with the government and to improve its level of professionalism is to enhance networking and coordination within the Japanese NGO community. One group that has taken a lead in this effort on the domestic front is Nippon Volunteer Network Active in Disasters, which grew out of the Kobe earthquake experience and has worked to coordinate partnerships with local governments, assist with local preparations and information awareness campaigns, coordinate volunteers, and share best practices among disaster response NGOs. Other, similar groups exist for domestic and international disaster management NGOs.[21] Human and financial resource limitations will restrict how much time the NGOs can dedicate to professional development and networking, which is why developing clear priorities is important.

An area of discussion that could be a high priority for government-NGO discussion is the identification of appropriate roles and responsibilities. Professionals from the government will clearly be responsible for law and order, command and control, and search and rescue operations, and they will probably play an important role in logistical support. But some logistical support could be provided by NGOs and the private sector, and they can certainly assist with the care and feeding of disaster victims, as well as with relatively simple cleanup tasks. Traditionally, the SDF has played a prominent role in the longer-term care of disaster victims, but momentum is shifting in such a way that the SDF is trying to bring its resources to bear during the immedi-

---

21   These include Japan Platform, the Japan NGO Center, and the Japan NGO Center for International Cooperation.

ate relief and rescue operations, while at the same time civil society in Japan is becoming more capable of assisting victims and helping with recovery efforts.

In a well-managed operation, Japanese NGOs and the private sector could perhaps be mobilized to help backfill for the SDF in the area of longer-term care and recovery while the SDF moves to develop more rapid reaction capabilities. Managed poorly, this kind of combined effort will perpetuate a situation similar to the one following the Niigata earthquake described by a workshop participant, where the SDF continued to prepare and serve meals to local victims long after volunteers could have taken over the task, as long as they had access to a steady supply of fresh food. Local citizens were grateful for the SDF's assistance, but in the future these communities might be better served by uniting with neighbors to help themselves as much as possible, and SDF personnel might be more effectively deployed to handle other tasks that only they are equipped to handle. This overall approach of improving communication and developing some degree of agreed-upon burden sharing and specialization is one that is revisited later in this report, as it has direct relevance to disaster relief CMCoord at an international level, as well as for U.S.-Japan cooperation within these multilateral networks.

CMCoord on the International Stage

The CMCoord issue takes on additional complexity and urgency in an international context, especially when relatively poor and hard-to-reach communities are overwhelmed by a disaster. As noted earlier, the number of actors in an international relief operation is generally much greater than in a domestic scenario, and communication and coordination are more difficult to carry out effectively. Moreover, as challenging as it is domestically for different agencies and departments to share and integrate response plans, it is near impossible to do so on an international scale. Potential locations or circumstances for large-scale disasters in third countries are too numerous to plan for productively. Perhaps the best that can be done is to consistently build awareness among likely affected and aid-giving nations and NGOs regarding how they operate and the capabilities they can offer. A central player in these situations is the United Nations and its related agencies, such as the World Food Program (WFP) and the UN High Commissioner for Refugees (UNHCR).

The United Nations
The United Nations has long been providing humanitarian assistance and coordinating the efforts of the international community to respond to natural disasters and complex emergencies that are beyond the capacities of an affected nation. In 1991, after the UN struggled to curb the Kurdish refugee crisis and other emergencies, the organization introduced a series of reform measures to strengthen its ability to coordinate

humanitarian action in the field. In 1998, OCHA was established, and the under secretary general for humanitarian affairs and emergency relief coordinator, as its head, was appointed to prepare for and oversee future UN relief operations.[22] The ERC chairs the key policy-making mechanisms in the HA/DR realm, including the IASC, which develops common guidelines and standards for humanitarian operations, and the Executive Committee for Humanitarian Affairs (ECHA), which develops common UN positions on humanitarian issues.[23] Operations in the field are managed through a network of field offices that support UN humanitarian coordinators (HCs) appointed to lead a particular relief effort along with country teams led by a resident coordinator (RC).[24] Regional support offices and regional disaster response advisors in Africa, the Caribbean and Latin America, the Middle East, and the Asia-Pacific area can also be called upon for assistance. Of course, in response to a disaster or humanitarian crisis, the affected nation always leads the relief operation, but OCHA assists by coordinating as much as possible the supporting relief efforts of the UN and international community, including national militaries, the private sector, and local and international NGOs. In addition, OCHA monitors and issues situation reports on emerging crises and natural disasters on a twenty-four hour basis through its network of information management services.[25] Today, OCHA has over fifteen hundred staff members across the globe and

---

22 The under secretary general for humanitarian affairs also serves as the emergency relief coordinator.

23 Membership on the IASC includes all UN operational humanitarian agencies, with standing invitations to participate sent to the International Committee of the Red Cross (ICRC), the International Federation of Red Cross and Red Crescent Societies (IFRC), the International Organization of Migration (IOM), the Office of the High Commissioner for Human Rights (OHCHR), the representative of the secretary-general on the human rights of internally displaced persons (IDPs), the World Bank, and three primary NGO consortia: the International Council of Voluntary Agencies (ICVA), InterAction, and the Steering Committee for Humanitarian Response (SCHR). The decision on whether and whom to appoint as humanitarian coordinator is made by the emergency relief coordinator, in consultation with the Inter-Agency Standing Committee.

24 The decision on whether and who to appoint as HC is made by the ERC, in consultation with the IASC.

25 OCHA administers several online information portals, such as ReliefWeb, the Integrated Regional Information Networks (IRIN), Virtual OSOCC, HumanitarianInfo.org, and OCHA On-line.

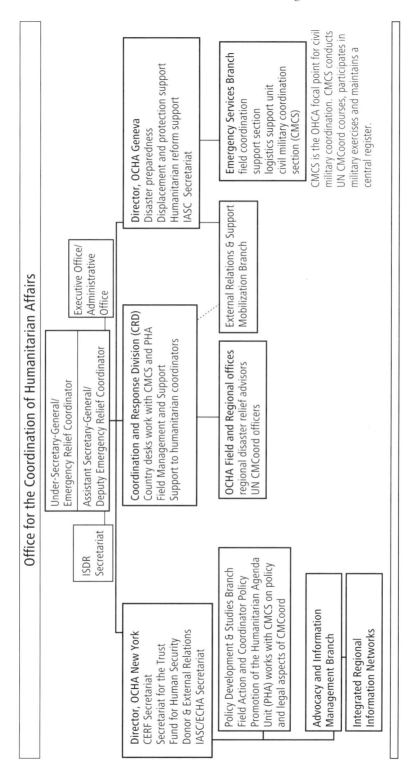

Office for the Coordination of Humanitarian Affairs

Under-Secretary-General/
Emergency Relief Coordinator

Assistant Secretary-General/
Deputy Emergency Relief Coordinator

Executive Office/
Administrative Office

ISDR Secretariat

Director, OCHA Geneva
Disaster preparedness
Displacement and protection support
Humanitarian reform support
IASC Secretariat

Emergency Services Branch
field coordination support section
logistics support unit
civil military coordination section (CMCS)

CMCS is the OHCA focal point for civil military coordination. CMCS conducts UN CMCoord courses, participates in military exercises and maintains a central register.

Coordination and Response Division (CRD)
Country desks work with CMCS and PHA
Field Management and Support
Support to humanitarian coordinators

External Relations & Support Mobilization Branch

OCHA Field and Regional offices
regional disaster relief advisors
UN CMCoord officers

Director, OCHA New York
CERF Secretariat
Secretariat for the Trust Fund for Human Security
Donor & External Relations
IASC/ECHA Secretariat

Policy Development & Studies Branch
Field Action and Coordinator Policy
Promotion of the Humanitarian Agenda
Unit (PHA) works with CMCS on policy and legal aspects of CMCoord

Advocacy and Information Management Branch

Integrated Regional Information Networks

maintains six regional offices, twenty field offices, two liaison offices, and headquarters (in New York and Geneva). OCHA's budget requirements for 2009 are $239 million, of which $12.3 million will come from the regular UN budget and the remainder from member states and donor organizations (OCHA 2009).

In response to a sudden natural disaster or humanitarian emergency, OCHA can deploy a special team of disaster management personnel within twelve to forty-eight hours. Managed by OCHA's Field Coordination Support Section (FCSS) in Geneva, a UN disaster assessment and coordination (UNDAC) team would rush to the site, assess the disaster situation, and assist local authorities in coordinating international response efforts. Most importantly, UNDAC teams run an on-site operations coordination center (OSOCC) and an internet-based virtual OSOCC (V-OSOCC) to facilitate the immediate exchange of information between responding governments and organizations during the relief operation. The FCSS also acts as the secretariat for the International Search and Rescue Advisory Group (INSARAG), a global network of urban search and rescue teams, and for the International Humanitarian Partnership (IHP) and the Asia-Pacific Humanitarian Partnership (APHP), which provide UNDAC teams with technical, logistics, and communications support modules and personnel during humanitarian missions.

Depending on the demands of the emergency, the ERC may also appoint an HC to serve as the most senior UN humanitarian official on the ground.[26] Since 1993, UNDAC has participated in nearly two hundred relief operations, including the Pakistan earthquake, hurricane Katrina, the Indian Ocean tsunami, and the Myanmar cyclone. The FCSS also conducts UNDAC training to increase interaction between OCHA staff and emergency managers from contributing member states, teach techniques on emergency response, and familiarize trainees with the UN system.

OCHA also administers ReliefWeb, which is an open, online gateway to relevant information, including situation reports and digital maps, on complex humanitarian emergencies and natural disasters worldwide.

---

26 This humanitarian coordinator is almost always the resident coordinator (RC), who is already serving as the senior UN official in the affected country. For extremely large-scale events, or if a disaster affects multiple countries simultaneously, a separate HC or regional HC is sometimes appointed.

Moreover, ReliefWeb provides twenty-four hour coverage of current re-lief, preparedness, and prevention activities as they unfold. The site's map center monitors ongoing HA/DR operations with satellite and dig-ital images, and then sorts and catalogues the data by country, region, or issue, including damage and needs assessments, food security, ref-ugee movement, and security. Additional OCHA online information tools include the Integrated Regional Information Networks (IRIN) news website and HumanitarianInfo.org, both of which post daily situation updates to keep relief workers and decision makers fully abreast of de-velopments across various disaster zones.

In addition, OCHA funds the Global Disaster Alert and Coordina-tion System (GDACS), a web-based platform that consolidates in one place a broad array of online disaster information management systems, including those referenced above, and also integrates those developed by other partner organizations, such as the United States Geological Survey (USGS). Pooling these diverse data streams, GDACS alerts the international community to natural, technological, and environmental disasters that occur worldwide, and provides information sharing and updating tools that are useful to response coordination during the imme-diate relief phase. This includes capabilities for tracking media reports, producing and cataloguing maps of the disaster zone and surround-ing areas, and linking to V-OSOCC discussion threads to allow disaster managers to exchange information, coordinate relief efforts, and ensure interoperability in near-real time. Finally, OCHA also offers OCHA On-line, an internet platform that (among other things) helps businesses identify ways in which they can help UN-sponsored relief efforts.

Of course, ready access to detailed satellite images and related geo-graphic information is enormously important for first responders as they struggle to understand and measure the scale and scope of a di-saster. Largely for this reason, the UN introduced its own satellite data service in the 1990s called UNOSAT to provide the international com-munity – especially developing countries with limited national means – with precisely this type of support. Based since 2002 at the Europe-an Organization for Nuclear Research (commonly referred to by its French acronym, CERN), UNOSAT works closely with UN field work-ers, satellite imagery experts, geographers, database programmers, and internet communications specialists to deliver images twenty-four hours a day through a web-based geographic interface or imagery data bank. On December 29, 2004, for example, three days after the tsunami tragedy, UNOSAT posted online and distributed to the field local and region-wide damage assessment maps retrieved from thirteen different satellites. These maps provided detailed measurements of the topography of the affected coastal areas, assisting relief workers in planning their responses. A UNOSAT report on roads and bridges damaged by the tsunami also proved to be extremely helpful in subsequent efforts to rebuild transportation networks (Hammerle and Cremel 2005).

In addition to the numerous information portals, OCHA's Logistics Support Unit (LSU) manages and tracks the procurement and delivery of emergency relief goods from OCHA stockpiles, which are located in the United Nations Humanitarian Response Depot (UNHRD) in Brindisi, Italy. The LSU also provides the broader international community with logistics-related support, such as facilitating customs operations, establishing common warehousing, identifying delivery routes, and managing transport schedules. In addition to the LSU, the UN Joint Logistics Center (UNJLC) provides logistical and supply-chain management support to UN agencies and to other humanitarian organizations responding to large-scale emergencies, such as the 2004 Indian Ocean tsunami and 2005 Pakistan earthquake, in order to meet host nation needs and prevent logistical bottlenecks or duplication.[27] If logistical activities will make up a significant part of an HA/DR mission, OCHA may deploy staff from the UNJLC within twenty-four hours of a crisis to help organize the logistics of the various relief organizations involved and to help coordinate with non-humanitarian agencies, such as the military.[28] The decision to send UNJLC staff depends on the scale of the crisis, the capabilities of relief agencies already involved, preliminary situation assessments, the extent of bottlenecks, and the possible use of military or civil defense assets (MCDA).

Once UNJLC becomes involved, its responsibilities include scheduling the movement of humanitarian cargo and relief workers within the

---

27   The UNJLC is an interagency logistics coordination facility for emergency response established in 2002 under the custodianship of the World Food Program (WFP). The UNJLC reports to the HC during a crisis and coordinates the logistics capabilities of humanitarian organizations involved in the operation.

28   Staffing is primarily handled through seconded staff from other humanitarian agencies within the UN system.

crisis area; managing the import, receipt, dispatch, and tracking of re-lief commodities; coordinating the use of available warehouse capacity; and, upon request, assessing the condition of roads, bridges, airports, ports, and other logistical infrastructure. Generally, the UNJLC website posts up-to-date information about the accessibility of entry points, customs and visa requirements, in-country warehousing availability, and appropriate contact information for commercial partners involved in the relief operation.

The UNJLC also maintains an air-operations cell to coordinate the use of all air assets made available under UN auspices for the common use of UN agencies, international organizations, and NGOs. Similarly, the United Nations Humanitarian Air Service (UNHAS) charters air-craft for either passenger or cargo operations. During the early stages of an emergency, UNHAS headquarters in Rome sends out an assessment team to evaluate the situation and assess local aviation infrastructure and fuel support.

The World Food Program, the administrator of both the UNJLC and UNHAS, drew on both units to launch two major operations during the 2004 tsunami to relieve airport congestion and to coordinate the receipt and delivery of relief supplies from the airfields to distribution points farther afield. The first operation provided logistical support to set up mobile storage tents and a base camp for relief workers in Banda Aceh, to facilitate the delivery of landing craft and water purification units, and to transport a mine action team to Sri Lanka. The second operation provided air support to the disaster region as a whole, including teams to manage aid distribution at key air terminals and a passenger service to ferry humanitarian personnel from country to country. In a similar vein, after the Pakistan earthquake, WFP aviation experts established a main office in Islamabad and sub-offices in Muzaffarabad, Bagh, and Chattaplain, all of which helped UNHAS to provide passenger service and air transport capacity for the delivery of food, medicine, and sup-port equipment. Given the constraints on road and rail access to isolated communities, UNHAS played an especially useful role in securing ad-ditional transport helicopters, including sixteen MI8s, two MI26s, two KA-32s, and four CH-47 *Chinooks* from the U.S. Army, two CH-53 H *Super Stallions* from Germany, and two UH-60 *Black Hawks* from the Austra-lian Army (Perry 2009, 106).

In response to the steady increase of military involvement and assets in support of humanitarian emergencies, OCHA released two documents to improve coordination among the myriad of actors involved, the *United Nations Civil-Military Coordination Officer Field Handbook* and the *Guidelines on the Use of MCDA in Disaster Relief* (Oslo Guidelines). Developed in 2008, the field handbook is designed to promote "the essential dialogue and interaction between civilian and military actors in humanitarian emergencies that is necessary to protect and promote humanitarian principles, avoid competition, minimize inconsistency, and when appropriate pursue common goals" (UN 2008b, iv). Specifically, the field handbook briefs humanitarian workers on the key military actors involved in security, medical evacuation, logistics, transport, communications, and information management. In addition, the handbook lists the lessons learned and best practices observed from past operations, such as the need to share routes and schedules for humanitarian convoys and to develop a common vocabulary between humanitarian aid workers and military actors. Finally, the handbook outlines the strategy and methods for establishing liaison with military forces at each stage of the operation.

Whenever MCDA are deployed in humanitarian emergencies, the Civil-Military Coordination Section (CMCS) is usually the OCHA focal point for integrating these components of the relief mission.[29] To ensure effective civil-military coordination in the field, the unit regularly conducts CMCoord courses and participates in military training exercises with other civil humanitarian actors. The unit also embeds CMCoord officers within deployed teams to serve as liaisons to governments, organizations, and militaries contributing to or requiring MCDA support during an operation. During the tsunami response, for example, OCHA had CMCoord officers in Sri Lanka (Colombo), Indonesia (Banda Aceh, Meuleboh, Medan, and Jakarta), and Thailand (Bangkok and Utapao).

In view of the steady increase of military involvement and assets in support of humanitarian emergencies and to improve consistency with other UN documents, the CMCS worked with other stakeholders to update the 1994 Oslo Guidelines in 2007. Updates to the guidelines continue

---

29 MCDA include standby relief personnel, equipment, supplies, and even services (such as weather reports) provided by foreign governments and militaries during a disaster relief operation.

Appropriate Relief Tasks of the Military Based on Mission

Availability and Impartiality of Forces

Humanitarian Tasks

Mission of Military →

Visibility of Task		Peaceful	Peacekeeping	Peace Enforcement	Combat
	Direct	Maybe	Maybe	No	No
	Indirect	Yes	Maybe	Maybe	No
	Infrastructure Support	Yes	Yes	Maybe	Maybe

Hierarchy of Assistance Tasks
Direct Assistance is the face-to-face distribution of goods and services.
Indirect Assistance is at least one step removed from the population and involves such activities as transporting relief goods or relief personnel.
Infrastructure Support involves providing general services, such as road repair, airspace management, and power generation that facilitate relief, but are not necessarily visible to or solely for the benefit of the affected population.

to emphasize the core principles of humanitarian assistance (humanity, neutrality, and impartiality) and define the types of humanitarian activities that are appropriate to support with international military resources. For example, the guidelines encourage military forces to provide infrastructure support such as road repair, power generation, and airspace management, but they discourage the direct distribution of goods and services by military personnel to the affected population, fearing such actions may blur the lines between the normal functions and roles of humanitarian and military stakeholders.

To keep these lines clear, the guidelines recommend that humanitarian actors maintain the lead role in humanitarian relief operations, particularly in areas also seized in conflict. "You need a long-term understanding of the situation on the ground in the affected country to recognize the potential impact of short-term actions, and NGOs and UN agencies will usually be better positioned on this front," advised one participant at IFPA's December 2006 workshop. As a result, the Oslo Guidelines emphasize the use of MCDA as a last resort when no other comparable civilian alternative exists and only when the use of military or civil defense assets can meet a critical humanitarian need. Of course, in recent years, the definition of "last resort" has evolved somewhat to consider other factors that favor prompt military assistance, such as the timeliness, appropriateness, and effectiveness of military assets, particularly during the first seventy-two hours of a crisis. As a result, the concept of last resort has become increasingly vague, raising numerous questions among practitioners. "The decision to involve MCDA can be made within a matter of hours. However, who decides when the military should step in? Who decides when there is an inadequate civilian capacity to respond? Is it the host nation or the international community?" questioned one participant at the 2008 workshop.

As the OCHA focal point for integrating the humanitarian and military components of the relief mission, the CMCS also administers the OCHA Central Register of Disaster Management Capacities, a database of personnel and disaster management assets within the UN system and from contributing governments and NGOs that could potentially be made available. The database includes directories on MCDA, emergency stockpiles of disaster relief material, donors of emergency humanitarian assistance, and contact points for disaster response, such as search and rescue experts. Unfortunately, the effectiveness of the database is questionable. Contributing nations usually prefer to channel their provision of military and civil defense assets to a disaster area via pre-negotiated bilateral arrangements with the affected countries or via separate stand-by agreements they may have established with regional organizations or even UN agencies. For instance, of the approximately thirty-five countries providing military assets during the tsunami relief effort, only two, Switzerland and Denmark, agreed to place their military assets under UN direction drawn from OCHA's central register. Switzerland provided three Super Puma helicopters, flight crew, logistics, and ground personnel, and Denmark offered a C-130 Hercules aircraft, flight crew, and some support personnel (Hobson 2005).

Unfortunately, the reluctance of donor states to put military assets under UN direction has complicated relief efforts in the past, particularly since national contributions to humanitarian operations are often not reported to the UN in the initial stages of the disaster response, making it difficult for UN officials to know precisely what assets are on site already and what else might be available. As a result, relief operations have suffered from logistical bottlenecks, duplication of assistance efforts in some locations, and supply shortages in other places. More-

ASEAN Standby Arrangements for Disaster Relief and Emergency Response	
Categories of information required to establish and maintain the inventory of earmarked assets and capacities for the regional standby arrangements	
Emergency Response / Search and Rescue	Military and Civilian Assets
Emergency Stockpiles of Disaster Relief Items	Disaster Management Expertise and Technologies

Source: ASEAN Secretariat

over, protracted negotiations between nations over the deployment of military and air relief operations, such as landing authorization and customs clearance, have also delayed the transit of goods and equipment for emergency assistance. Still, one must keep in mind the need for speed in these situations, so it is often useful for donor countries to provide military resources quickly on their own initiative, rather than wait for a central coordinating group to mobilize, assess, and request specific assistance.

In an effort to bridge this gap, the UN Joint Inspection Unit has recommended that the UN review existing rules and guiding principles on international humanitarian assistance in order to help formulate an international framework for disaster response.[30] In theory, establishing a set of regulatory norms and legal instruments on disaster management that disaster-affected countries and assisting governments and relief agencies would agree to apply on the ground would certainly enhance the efficiency of relief operations. However, accomplishing this could take many years, given the number of potential players involved, if it is even possible. In the short term, assisting a core group of member states in establishing standby arrangements among their national civil and military stakeholders in order to improve bilateral and multilateral disaster assistance and coordination mechanisms is a more manageable undertaking. The Association of Southeast Asian Nations (ASEAN) has already begun its own disaster relief standby arrangement process, based on an ASEAN agreement signed in July 2005. Harmonizing policies and procedures among close allies and regional groupings would improve how these partners cooperate as members of a UN or multilat-

---

30   The Joint Inspection Unit is an external oversight body of the UN, mandated to conduct evaluations and investigations of the UN system.

eral coalition, as well as pave the way for later achieving an international regulatory framework on disaster response and recovery. The United States and Japan can provide leadership in this area.

The United States and Japan already have in place the Acquisition and Cross-Servicing Agreement, which governs the reciprocal provision of logistics support and supplies between the SDF and U.S. armed forces for bilateral exercises and training, humanitarian international relief operations, UN peacekeeping operations (PKO), and operations in response to an armed attack against Japan.[31] This is a good start, but it does not yet take into account the non-military side of the equation and it is not yet easily extended to other countries. Improving the ability of the United States and Japan to pool their civilian and military resources in response to domestic or international large-scale disasters will not only strengthen linkages between the two countries, but also improve how the two coordinate their efforts with the United Nations.

Establishing standby arrangements between the UN and individual member states is yet another way to enhance UN access to MCDA for humanitarian operations. In fact, the UN already has such an arrangement in place for peacekeeping operations: the United Nations Stand-by Arrangement System (UNSAS). As part of UNSAS, participating member states pledge to maintain and make available specified resources (military formations, civilian and military personnel, material and equipment, or support assets) for use by the UN Department of Peacekeeping. Of course, the final decision to actually deploy these resources remains a national decision. However, when deployed, these resources are under the operational control of the United Nations. In 2009, UNSAS had eighty-seven members, including Australia, Canada, China, France, the Republic of Korea, India, Russia, Singapore, the United Kingdom, and the United States.[32] Japan announced in July 2009 that it would join the system.

---

31 The Acquisition and Cross-Servicing Agreement between the United States and Japan enables the two countries to exchange logistics support and supplies and services, including food, fuel, transportation, ammunition, equipment, base support, medical services, and use of airport and seaport services.

32 Member states pledge to UNSAS at four different commitment levels: Level 1 requires member states to simply identify their capabilities. Level 2 members must provide an inventory list detailing the types of contributions available for use, including the organization of units, a list of major equipment, and data on personnel.

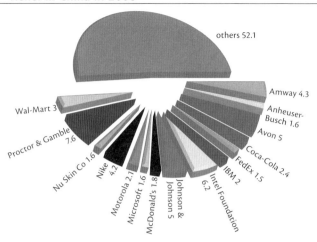

U.S. Corporate Donations to Earthquake
Relief in China in 2008

others 52.1

Amway 4.3

Anheuser-Busch 1.6

Avon 5

Coca-Cola 2.4

FedEx 1.5

IBM 2

Intel Foundation 6.2

Johnson & Johnson 5

McDonald's 1.8

Microsoft 1.6

Motorola 2.1

Nike 4.2

Nu Skin Co 1.6

Proctor & Gamble 7.6

Wal-Mart 3

$102 million total   *Figures in millions of $US. Contributions over $1.5m broken out.*

If member states can make conditional commitments to the UN for peacekeeping operations, it should be possible to establish a similar arrangement for HA/DR activities, particularly in the area of infrastructure support. The same is true for the private sector, and some progress has been made in this area. The package delivery company DHL, for example, signed a memorandum of understanding with OCHA in 2006 to assist with logistics. Both peacekeeping and disaster response missions require military and civilian agents to deliver daily necessities, repair damaged infrastructure, protect displaced persons, offer medical assistance, and provide security; adapting UNSAS for disaster relief operations (perhaps a more robust version of OCHA's Central Register of Disaster Management Capabilities) could enhance the capacity for international disaster response and promote greater coordination among participating member states.

Level 3 members have signed general memorandums of understanding (MOUs) or standby arrangements with the UN specifying all available resources, response times, and conditions for employment. Finally, level 4 members have signed specific MOUs that contain agreements on contingent owned equipment. Level 4 cannot be attained until after detailed negotiations with the member state, including visits. China, the Republic of Korea, and the United States are level 1 member states. Australia and India are level 2 member states, and Canada, France, Russia, Singapore, and the United Kingdom are level 3 member states.

In addition to improving the UN's resource capacity through bilateral and multilateral standby arrangements, strengthening civil-military coordination mechanisms (such as joint training, shared communication networks, and liaison officers) may also help to improve the UN's capability for rapid response, as well as to minimize the cultural divide between civil and military partners in approaching HA/DR activities, including differences in exit strategies, command structures, and needs assessments. Indeed, matching resources to local needs is a significant challenge for first responders, particularly for military forces normally equipped for combat support missions. A U.S. military review of the relief operation in Pakistan stated, "The biggest challenge noted early on was the lack of a clear, common situational understanding of the humanitarian needs and outstanding requirements. This led to inefficient use of resources and an excess of aid resources arriving in more accessible areas while insufficient amounts reached areas that were less accessible or cut off" (Center for Excellence in Disaster Management and Humanitarian Assistance 2006).

Though a lack of local capacity and information awareness during the early days of a response often necessitates a "supply push" system, in which external responders assume what kind of assistance is required and push it out, the UN and other humanitarian groups believe that the most effective humanitarian operations over the long term are "demand pull" systems dictated by sector-based needs (Hobson 2005). To help negotiate the transition from push to pull and to strengthen overall cooperation in the field, the UN conducted a series of reviews on humanitarian action. The tsunami response experience revealed weaknesses in the coordination of military assets and logistics, as well as gaps in capacity and communications in sectors such as water and sanitation, shelter and camp management, and recovery.

As a result of these reviews, the UN developed a new framework for dividing different aspects of a relief operation into clusters of similarly engaged humanitarian agencies to respond in particular sectors of activity, with each sector having a clear and accountable lead. These are not unlike ESFs in the United States, though they are fewer in number. By mapping the response capacities of national, regional, and international actors, the UN grouped civil and military stakeholders into clusters dealing with services (logistics and emergency telecommunications), relief and assistance (emergency shelter, health, nutrition, water, sanitation and hygiene, and education), or crosscutting issues (early recovery and protection).

The Pakistan earthquake presented an opportunity to introduce the cluster approach as the new UN framework for coordinating emergency response, even though it was not yet fully developed. Within twenty-four hours of the disaster, OCHA established nine clusters in Islamabad: food and nutrition; water and sanitation; health; telecommunications; emergency shelter; early recovery and reconstruction; logistics; camp management and protection; and education (ActionAid International 2006). Each of the four regional UNDAC field presences also established cluster sites, called humanitarian hubs. Initially, clusters were only intended to fill gaps between sector responsibilities, but as the emergency progressed, the number of clusters and sub-clusters grew exponentially, making it difficult for stakeholders to harmonize tasks and avoid duplication and overlap. A UN assessment of the cluster approach later acknowledged that "Inter-cluster coordination was deficient as was the lack of a nexus between field hubs and Islamabad" (Inter-Agency Standing Committee 2006, 3).

Poor coordination and weak information management, compounded by unclear terms of references, vague exit strategies for clusters, over-centralized decision making, insufficient support and training, and high turnover among UN staff, hindered the effectiveness of the cluster approach in Pakistan. Limited engagement with local NGOs and civil society further frustrated relief and recovery efforts, prompting many to criticize the cluster approach as being too "UN centric" and an "exclusive club" (Inter-Agency Standing Committee 2006, 9).

Yet despite these shortcomings, the UN concluded that the "cluster approach did successfully provide a single and recognizable framework for coordination, collaboration, decision-making, and practical solutions in a chaotic operational environment" (Inter-Agency Standing Committee 2006, 9). UN engagement with the Pakistani military and national government was strong, which helped promote full government ownership of the clusters. OCHA co-chaired cluster meetings with government representatives and worked closely with the army to ensure that sufficient humanitarian assistance reached even the most remote areas of Pakistan. In the end, the cluster system was considered useful in that "it

UN Response To Pakistan Earthquake The Cluster Approach	
UN Cluster	**Managing UN Agency**
Relief and Assistance	
Emergency Shelter	IOM, UNHCR, UNDP
Health	WHO, UNICEF, UNFPA
Nutrition	WFP, UNICEF
Water, Sanitation & Hygiene	UNICEF
Services	
Logistics	WFP
Emergency Telecommunications	WFP
Cross-cutting Issues	
Early Recovery	UNDP
Camp Coordination and Management	UNHCR, IOM, UNDP
Protection	UNHCR, UNICEF
Education	UNICEF, UNESCO
Operational Hubs	
Bagh	Mansehra
Batagram	Muzaffarabad
Logistics Hubs	
Abbotabad	Islamabad
Bagh	Kahuta
Batagram	Mansehra
Chatter Plain	Muzaffarabad
Garhi Habibullah	

Source: "Pakistan: UN Achievements – One Year Later," ReliefWeb, October 9, 2006, available at http://www.reliefweb.int/rw/rwb.nsf/db900sid/EGUA-6UELKY?OpenDocument

developed to become an important organizing mechanism," according to one U.S. military assessment (Center for Excellence in Disaster Management and Humanitarian Assistance 2006). A workshop participant remarked, "The key to making the clusters work was leadership. Some were run mainly from the perspective of the lead agency or were poorly managed, while others were able to efficiently coordinate the contributions of all the members."

In addition to identifying capacity gaps, the cluster approach is a tool for UN agencies, foreign militaries, local and international NGOs, and private-sector donors to operate as partners. "We need to create familiarity in the field. The military needs to understand how the UN and NGO communities operate. They are the military's exit strategy," recommended one workshop participant. "The cluster system provides a logistical structure for the military to plug into," added another participant. Integrating response strategies in this way allows stakeholders to focus on areas where they have a comparative advantage (security, logistics, and transport for militaries and recovery and rehabilitation for aid workers), thus ensuring the military and civilian components of HA/DR activities remain distinct. The clusters also create a smaller pool of responsible people to work with, which makes it easier for the different organizations to develop personal and institutional relationships. In view of these advantages, UN authorities and the broader humanitarian relief community (including HA/DR experts in the military) will continue to refine the cluster concept and to promote it as an integral tool for improving disaster responses in the years ahead. In fact, the clusters now authorized by the IASC have emerged as logical points of entry into the HA/DR network for U.S. and foreign militaries, NGOs, and private sector companies that seek a more prominent and effective role in disaster relief.[33]

Although the cluster approach potentially enhances humanitarian cooperation during a HA/DR operation, the level of participation and coordination between civil and military partners in these clusters depends largely on the amount of resources and time devoted to joint planning, training, and exercises before the onset of a crisis. Coordinated planning between militaries and civil agents for disaster response will also help standardize data management and reporting techniques among stakeholders in order to better identify logistical needs during a disaster and also address common communication challenges, such as military classification policies and incompatible communication systems (such as mobile phones and e-mail accounts versus fax communications). The further development of existing programs, such as UNDAC and INSARAG training, CMCoord courses, and other bilateral and multinational exercises and courses, should be leveraged to help improve civil-military coordination for future operations. One workshop participant weary of seeing individual countries take steps to upgrade their military and national response plans for HA/DR activities without coordinating with the UN advised, "At the end of the day, we need to integrate our planning efforts and adopt a holistic approach to humanitarian action. Let us not politicize civil-military coordination. By doing so, we destroy it."

---

33   Cluster leads include the IFRC, the IOM, the United Nations Development Program (UNDP), UNHCR, the United Nations Children's Fund (UNICEF), OHCHR, OCHA, the WFP, and the World Health Organization (WHO).

The United States

The United States has consistently contributed to international disaster relief operations over many years. The Department of State serves as the U.S. lead federal agency (LFA) for non-military incidents abroad, relying on the regional bureau responsible for the area where the disaster has struck and on USAID/OFDA to coordinate the overall response. Once the government of the disaster-stricken nation has requested assistance, the U.S. embassy in the affected nation reaches out immediately to the Operations Center (a small room in the Harry S. Truman Building packed with chairs, computers, phones, and faxes) within the Executive Secretariat of the State Department via a disaster declaration cable.[34] For large-scale events, the local U.S. ambassador will probably also contact the relevant U.S. military regional combatant command (COCOM), such as U.S. Pacific Command (PACOM) in Honolulu. For its part, the Operations Center, which maintains a twenty-four hour watch on emerging or rapid-onset crises overseas, will quickly set up an IASC led by the appropriate regional bureau to monitor the situation and facilitate interagency coordination.[35]

In addition to staff from the regional bureau, the IASC generally includes representatives from the bureaus of political-military affairs, consular affairs, diplomatic security, and public affairs, as well as personnel from USAID, the National Security Council (NSC), and the departments of Agriculture, Health and Human Services, and Defense. Each agency and department establishes parallel departmental JTFs that are linked to the White House and all other relevant agencies through the Operations Center. Given the numbers involved, managing and directing the interactions among all the relevant offices and agencies can be a time-consuming and labor-intensive process, especially during major disasters. In the tsunami case, the Operations Center was on alert twenty-four hours a day for seventeen days, with over 280 people rotating through in shifts. The NSC also chaired a daily video conference

---

34   Under U.S. law, to set a formal disaster relief operation in motion, the cable must meet three criteria: 1) the disaster must be beyond the ability of the host nation to handle on its own; 2) the host nation must formally request U.S. assistance; and 3) such assistance must be in the strategic interests of the United States (which is almost always the case).

35   The State Department's lead-agency role for non-military incidents was confirmed in presidential directive/NSC-27, January 19, 1978.

with the various JTF heads that focused on operational issues, led by the NSC's director for humanitarian assistance and disaster relief in the International Economic Affairs section.[36]

Generally, the secretary of defense orders the deployment of military assets during large-scale disasters. An intense period of consultation often ensues among the embassy, State, OFDA, the regional command, and the Office of the Secretary of Defense to determine the extent of the operation and the optimal military deployment, which is then formalized in a written State Department request submitted to the Pentagon.

The formal U.S. process for approving foreign disaster relief efforts and, most specifically, military support, however, often has been bypassed in favor of an informal, back-channel process that is not always well informed or consistent. In certain situations, local U.S. ambassadors in disaster-stricken countries have reached out directly to the regional COCOM to request military assistance well before the interagency coordination process has begun in earnest, sometimes leaving OFDA in the dark. Moreover, some officials at State are neither familiar with disaster management issues and procedures nor even aware of USAID's and OFDA's role as the LFA for foreign HA/DR activities. For instance, in response to flash floods in the Horn of Africa in 2006, State issued a request for DoD assistance. When personnel from DoD spoke with the relevant regional bureau at State, they found that staffs at the bureau were unaware of OFDA's role or that USAID was in fact the LFA. Still worse, DoD actually had to give bureau officials the contact information for the proper USAID/OFDA representatives (interview 2007a). At other times, regional COCOM commanders, eager to be responsive and demonstrate goodwill, have deployed forces to a disaster zone and prepared to provide assistance well beyond the levels they are allowed without prior DoD approval, and before OFDA and others in the Pentagon have determined that such assistance is necessary and appropriate. In recent years, new procedures and organizational structures, outlined below, were introduced largely because of the 2004 tsunami and 2005

---

36   This approach to the management of a "complex contingency operation" is similar to that outlined in the May 1997 Presidential Decision Directive (PDD) 56, in which the deputy secretaries of relevant departments established appropriate interagency working groups (normally an executive committee at the assistant secretary level) to supervise the day-to-day management of the operation.

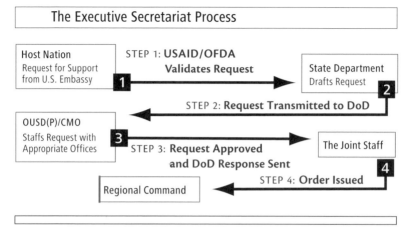

The Executive Secretariat Process

Host Nation
Request for Support from U.S. Embassy
1

STEP 1: **USAID/OFDA**
Validates Request

State Department
Drafts Request
2

STEP 2: **Request Transmitted to DoD**

OUSD(P)/CMO
Staffs Request with Appropriate Offices
3

STEP 3: **Request Approved**
and DoD Response Sent

The Joint Staff
4

STEP 4: **Order Issued**

Regional Command

earthquake experiences to improve the formal U.S. process for approving foreign disaster relief efforts and, most specifically, military support.

As mentioned, the U.S. embassy in the affected nation reaches out to the Operations Center within the Executive Secretariat of the State Department via a disaster declaration cable. If it is determined that military assets are needed to respond to a disaster, OFDA will submit a formal request for military assistance to the State Department's Executive Secretariat, which will in turn forward the request to the Executive Secretariat of DoD. Upon receiving the request for assistance, the Executive Secretariat at DoD forwards the request to the office of Coalition and Multinational Operations (CMO), a sub-branch of the Office of the Under Secretary of Defense for Policy (OUSD(P)). Through an intra-DoD review process that it manages, CMO collaborates with other DoD offices, including the appropriate regional desk, the Joint Staff, the Office of the Comptroller, Legal Affairs, and the Defense Security Cooperation Agency (DSCA), to organize and propose (or not) a military response. Even in cases involving a large-scale disaster and the prospect of major military commitment, this review can generally be done within two to three hours, after which a draft plan is sent back up the chain of command for final approval by the secretary and/or deputy secretary of defense.

Once the approval to send military assets is given, the Joint Staff orders the proper regional COCOM, and if necessary, a functional COCOM, such as Transportation Command (TRANSCOM), to respond to the crisis and provide both humanitarian assistance and any needed on-site organizational support. Meanwhile, the DoD Executive Secretariat and the CMO office will have been coordinating planning efforts via informal back channels with the State Department and the local U.S. embassy, to determine the optimal military deployment. In response to a disaster in the Asia-Pacific region, timely and effective U.S.-Japan communication during this brief stage in the process should help to make deployments more compatible and reduce redundancy. To the extent that U.S. assets are pulled from bases in Japan, it will also help to ensure that defense capabilities are maintained.

Meanwhile, in the field, USAID works closely with the U.S. embassy and the local USAID mission in the affected country (assuming that USAID has a mission there) to assess the humanitarian situation and determine priority needs. Within USAID, OFDA is the primary party responsible for coordinating the U.S. government response to both natural and man-made disasters overseas, including those arising from civil conflict, acts of terrorism, or industrial accidents. As far as disaster relief operations are concerned, OFDA actually serves as the operational-level LFA within the broader State Department community. Within twenty-four hours of a disaster declaration, OFDA provides up to $50,000 to the U.S. ambassador in the affected country for the purchase of local relief supplies (USAID OFDA 2006, 10), though this amount can be quickly increased to $100,000 without much difficulty. If necessary, OFDA may deploy a regional advisor and a DART team to the affected area to conduct rapid assessments of the disaster situation, analyze the existing capacity of the host nation and other relief agencies. OFDA also may coordinate operations on the ground with the affected country, other private donors and international organizations, and, when present, U.S. and foreign militaries.

Unlike the debate on civil-military coordination and the role of the military in response to domestic incidents, U.S. policy makers are generally more willing to mobilize military assets for overseas relief missions, as well as to give DoD relatively wide latitude to work directly with its military counterpart in the affected nation, especially when that nation lies within a region of strategic interest, as was the case during the 2004 Indian Ocean tsunami, the 2005 Pakistan earthquake, and the 2006 Philippines mudslide. With regard to those disasters, the rapid and massive military response was as much an opportunity to restore the U.S. public image, win hearts and minds, and further U.S. foreign policy goals, as it was a humanitarian call to deliver assistance and save lives. Indeed, retired General John Abizaid, former commander of U.S. Central Command (CENTCOM), reportedly acknowledged that the decision to launch a massive military relief effort in Pakistan was spurred by national security reasons in addition to humanitarian concerns. According to one participant at the December 2006 workshop, "What we're doing [in Pakistan] is just as important as what we're doing in Iraq and Afghanistan in the global war on terror."

That said, the humanitarian imperative is still paramount in these cases. "You don't go into something like this thinking about what impact it will have on our image," remarked Rear Admiral LeFever, USN, former commander of joint task force Disaster Assistance Center Pakistan (DAC). "You go into it focusing on doing the right thing to help people" (Braithwaite 2007). The U.S. military has rapid reaction and follow-on capabilities, such as emergency medical capabilities and sealift for heavy-volume equipment, and can provide a range of technical support, mobility, and lift capacity to improve the delivery of assistance to the affected nation. Moreover, many U.S. military assets are forward deployed and able to respond to a crisis within forty-eight hours. During the response to the Pakistan earthquake, for example, U.S. military assets, most notably its fleet of high altitude, heavy lift CH-47 Chinooks (often referred to as "angels of mercy" by the local population) were indispensable to local responders in their efforts to deliver assistance, provide shelter, conduct medical evacuations, and distribute relief supplies to remote villages (IFPA-OSIPP 2006).

Whatever the motivation behind deploying military resources to respond to large-scale disasters overseas, the challenges associated with these missions are constant. Chief among them is training personnel to understand and interact efficiently with all of the complex moving parts that make up such an operation (both domestically and internationally). As noted earlier, OFDA is a key U.S. government responder to international disasters and crises. OFDA staff work around the clock to monitor global hazards and potential areas of need, and OFDA teams include specialists from a variety of disciplines, including experts in disaster relief planning, damage assessment, search and rescue, water and sanitation, nutrition, shelter, logistics, contracting, communications, and medicine.

Moreover, OFDA works in close cooperation with other parts of USAID, such as the Office of Conflict Management and Mitigation and the Office of Private and Voluntary Cooperation, bilateral and multilateral donors, OCHA, and other U.S. government agencies that provide humanitarian assistance, including the departments of agriculture, health and human services, and defense. In catastrophic emergencies, OFDA deploys a DART team to an affected area to conduct rapid assessments of the disaster situation, analyze the existing capacity of the host nation and other relief agencies, and coordinate U.S. government relief efforts with the affected country, other private donors and international organizations, and, when they are present, U.S. and foreign militaries.

During the 2004 Indian Ocean tsunami response, OFDA dispatched over fifty-five DART members and one hundred field-based USAID staff to India, Indonesia, the Maldives, Sri Lanka, and Thailand. Through fifteen airlifts of emergency relief commodities, OFDA delivered hygiene kits to meet the emergency needs of more than 80,000 people, water containers for over 143,000 people, and emergency medical kits from the World Health Organization (WHO) with sufficient supplies for 10,000 people for three months (USAID OFDA 2005, 16). In addition, OFDA partners, which included over fifty NGOs and UN agencies, provided employment to over 70,000 people through cash-for-work activities, such as waste management, debris removal, and shelter construction.[37] In total, OFDA funds to local and international NGOs and UN agencies providing relief to tsunami-affected countries reached $84 million (USAID OFDA 2005, 17).

Over fifteen thousand U.S. soldiers and sailors also worked alongside OFDA during the tsunami response. The U.S. military deployed twenty-six ships, eighty-two planes, and fifty-one helicopters to help deliver more than 24.5 million tons of relief supplies and enable USAID and other relief agencies to move relief items to inaccessible areas (USAID OFDA 2005, 17). The U.S. Navy hospital ship USNS *Mercy* also arrived off the coast of Banda Aceh and personnel onboard performed over twenty thousand medical procedures. Moreover, the U.S. military facilitated a six-day, interagency, multi-sector assessment of the disaster situation

---

37   OFDA partners included CARE, CRS, IRC, IFRC, UNICEF, WHO, Mercy Corps, IMC, World Vision, CHF International, and the Asia Foundation, to name a few.

to provide the humanitarian community with a baseline from which to measure the impact of the relief and recovery programming.

As no two disasters are alike, DARTs generally are tailored and scaled to the crisis at hand, drawing in non-State Department experts as required. The response to tropical cyclone Sidr that hit Bangladesh in November 2007, for example, was far more limited in scale and timeframe than the response to the tsunami or Pakistan earthquake. Nonetheless, a five-person DART team was dispatched the day after the storm, and USAID/OFDA provided emergency funds for much-needed fresh water supplies and for airlifting plastic sheeting, hygiene and sanitation kits, and medical supplies to key distribution points. In early March 2008, a similarly small but essential response to heavy flooding in Ecuador involved a single C-130 cargo plane (from the Kentucky Air National Guard) delivering some 162 flood cleanup kits, 9,000 alcohol pads, 2,250 biohazard waste bags, and 9,000 disposable vinyl gloves.

All requests for assistance from OFDA staff and DARTs in the field are relayed to an on-call response management team (RMT) in charge of emergency operations based back in Washington. Logistics officers from the RMT coordinate the delivery of initial relief supplies, such as plastic sheeting, hygiene kits, health supplies, water containers and purification units, and blankets, from one of OFDA's commodity stockpiles located in Dubai, Italy, and Miami. The RMT also serves as the logistics liaison to other crisis centers and task forces involved in a U.S. government response, including the State Department's IASC. Project officers in Washington also review and fund flash appeals from partners in the field, mostly UN agencies and NGOs active in disaster-prone areas, such as UNICEF, CARE, and the International Federation of Red Cross and Red Crescent Societies.

In an effort to formalize a working relationship with U.S. and foreign militaries during disaster relief operations, OFDA often deploys military liaison officers to the field and to the relevant COCOM to coordinate activities between OFDA and military responders. In 2005, USAID established the Office of Military Affairs (OMA) as the focal point for USAID interaction with military planners during disaster response activities and stability operations. To date, OMA has facilitated the establishment of a joint USAID and DoD emergency supply warehouse in Bulgaria, provided pre-deployment briefings to U.S. military units en route to Afghanistan, Iraq, and the Philippines, and served as a liaison between the humanitarian community and DoD during disaster response efforts in Pakistan. USAID also updated its *Field Operations Guide for Disaster Assessment and Response* in September 2005, which included reference material for OFDA staff working with U.S., coalition, and multinational military forces, including NATO. While OMA tends to focus on policy issues related to U.S. CMCoord, another group within OFDA concentrates on the operational aspects. This group, the Operational Liaison Unit (OLU), conducts joint humanitarian operations training courses in cooperation with the U.S. military regional commands, and it dispatches CMCoord officers to onsite locations to assist with coordination in actual relief efforts. Senior USAID staff are assigned as well to regional COCOMs, especially those – such as PACOM and Southern Command (SOUTHCOM) – that oversee defense operations in disaster-prone areas.

Though not specifically charged with responding to global disasters, S/CRS is another State Department office with its hand in CMCoord policy issues. As mentioned earlier, the Bush administration established this office in 2004 to institutionalize the civilian capacity of the U.S. government to prepare for and respond to post-conflict crises and to help provide military personnel with a viable exit strategy. The S/CRS interagency team includes staff from USAID, DoD, U.S. Army Corps of Engineers, the Joint Chiefs of Staff, and the departments of Justice and Treasury. S/CRS also participates in military training exercises and plans to deploy humanitarian, stabilization, and reconstruction teams (HSRTs) to regional combatant commands during operations to facilitate the integration of civilian planning into military campaigns.

Of course, initiatives to enhance CMCoord for disaster relief operations will be inadequate if similar efforts are not made to improve how State's regional bureaus and its Executive Secretariat coordinate disaster relief efforts with USAID/OFDA. In this sense, intra-State coordination is just as important an objective as interagency coordination. One step toward that goal was taken in January 2006, when the secretary of state created the Office of the Director of Foreign Assistance (DFA) as a way to align more effectively the foreign assistance activities promoted and carried out by various main State Department offices and those of USAID (which is better seen as an independent agency that reports to

State). The DFA has authority over most State and USAID foreign assistance programs and provides guidance to other agencies that manage foreign aid activities.[38] The DFA also serves concurrently as the USAID administrator.

In May 2007, USAID and State jointly released their Strategic Plan for FY 2007-12, which defined the primary aims of U.S. foreign development assistance as 1) achieving peace and security, 2) supporting just and democratic governance, 3) investing in people, 4) promoting economic growth and prosperity, 5) providing humanitarian assistance, 6) promoting international understanding, and 7) strengthening U.S. consular and management capabilities (U.S. Department of State and U.S. Agency for International Development 2007, 10). With regard to providing humanitarian assistance, the new framework proposed to provide life-saving disaster relief assistance in emergencies, prevent and mitigate disasters by developing local and global mechanisms to anticipate and respond to natural or man-made disasters, and help build the capacity of foreign governments to manage problems associated with displaced persons and refugees. To accomplish this, the Strategic Plan identified the Departments of Homeland Security, Health and Human Services, and Defense as key government partners with which State and USAID plan to coordinate to implement future foreign assistance activities.

At this point, it is unclear whether these and other recent efforts to restructure the cumbersome and fragmented U.S. foreign assistance program will improve once and for all how State coordinates future HA/DR efforts with USAID. Some argue that since the DFA also serves as USAID administrator, USAID will likely participate in the policy and budget decision-making process to a greater extent than it does at present (Veillette 2007, 2). On the other hand, some critics fear that the role of USAID is being steadily marginalized in favor of the Department of State, with some of its responsibilities being usurped by main State bureaus and offices. Either way, State and USAID need to improve internal HA/DR procedures so that both are operating with the same understanding and assumptions when it is time to turn to the military for additional disaster relief assistance.

---

38   Some foreign aid programs, such as the Millennium Challenge Account, the Office of the Global AIDS Coordinator, and the Office for Reconstruction and Stabilization, remain outside the scope of the DFA.

For its part, the U.S. military is exploring various ways to enhance military readiness for and involvement in HA/DR activities. In late 2005, for example, after the Pakistan earthquake, the Pentagon introduced DoD directive 3000.05, "Military Support for Stability, Security, Transition, and Reconstruction (SSTR) Operations," which essentially elevated stability operations to a core military mission comparable to traditional combat missions.[39] This new doctrine incorporates S/CRS, USAID, other U.S. government departments, international organizations, foreign governments, and nonprofit and private sector organizations into planning efforts for stability operations. Simply put, the directive makes the provision of military aid in support of HA/DR-related programs a central DoD policy objective.

However, much remains to be done to educate defense officials and military commanders on the strategic value of such missions, how best to implement them in concert with non-DoD civilian authorities, and what the implications might be for force structure and military procurement. Moreover, so anomalous was this directive with traditional DoD policy, because it assigned some responsibilities to the U.S. military normally carried out by the Department of State and other civilian agencies, that it prompted the immediate release of a national security presidential directive by the White House (NSPD-44) to clarify State's overall primacy. NSPD-44 was titled "Management of Interagency Efforts Concerning Reconstruction and Stabilization," and it identified the Department of State as the main body "to coordinate and lead integrated United States government efforts, involving all U.S. departments and agencies with relevant capabilities to prepare, plan for, and conduct stabilization and reconstruction activities" (White House 2005).

Harmonizing policy in Washington, however, does not guarantee effective civil-military coordination in the field, particularly as the role (and budget) of the military expands in the area of foreign assistance. To ensure that the lines of authority between State and Defense do not

---

39   DoD's formal definition describes "stability operations" as an overarching term encompassing various military missions, tasks, and activities conducted outside the United States in coordination with other instruments of national power to maintain or reestablish a safe and secure environment and to provide essential government services, emergency infrastructure reconstruction, and humanitarian assistance, of which disaster relief is an integral part (U.S. Joint Chiefs of Staff 2006).

become blurred, members of the Senate Foreign Relations Committee visited selected embassies around the world to assess the two departments' coordinating efforts on the ground. In several cases, the committee found that military-conducted humanitarian and civic projects, such as the delivery of medical care and the construction of transportation systems, sanitation facilities, and schools, were carried out with limited embassy oversight or approval. "One ambassador lamented that his effectiveness in representing the U.S. to foreign officials was beginning to wane as more resources were being directed to military projects in the country" (U.S. Senate Committee on Foreign Relations 2006, 12).

In an effort to maximize coordination and efficiency, the committee also recommended that all ambassadors pursue MOUs, as some already have, regarding the military presence to clarify lines of authority. The committee also recommended that ambassadors have the authority to approve all military-related programs implemented in the country where they serve, and that the secretary of state administer all foreign assistance funding, including that authorized through defense budgets.

On the other hand, as requests for U.S. military and broader DoD assistance in support of foreign disaster relief have steadily risen in recent years, so has the need to ensure that those requests are grounded in sound strategic assessments, communicated to DoD in a useable format, and based on a demonstrated need for unique military capabilities. All too often, State Department officials or local U.S. ambassadors will simply request a specific type and scale of military support (for example, sea-based transport helicopters for evacuating disaster victims) without thinking through the logistical support required to make that capability available, or the possible availability of more cost-effective (possibly private sector) alternatives. Rising interest in "getting the request process right" (which DoD officials believe would resolve at least 70 percent of the difficulties that bedevil the current process) coincided with a wholesale reorganization of the OUSD(P) in January 2007. The reorganization was meant to address the department's growing emphasis on managing international military coalitions, equipping partner nations to fight terrorists, and improving U.S. and coalition responses to sudden disasters and humanitarian crises. Additional adjustments were made when the Obama administration took over in 2009.

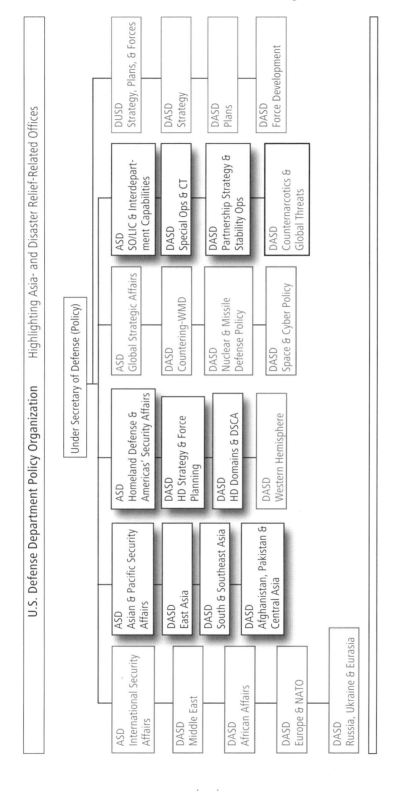

U.S. Defense Department Policy Organization   Highlighting Asia- and Disaster Relief-Related Offices

As part of this reorganization, a number of new assistant and deputy assistant secretary of defense positions were established, such as an assistant secretary of defense for Asian and Pacific security affairs and one for special operations/low-intensity conflict (SO/LIC) and interdependent capabilities. Serving under this latter post is a deputy assistant secretary for partnership strategy and stability operations, which is the primary office for foreign disaster relief (with the appropriate regional office), dealing with UN PKO and other operations, security cooperation planning, and interagency coordination. This organizational structure is much more centralized than in the past, and together the new offices share responsibility for organizing the DoD response to natural or man-made disasters in the Asia-Pacific region. These organizational changes have in turn prompted a top-to-bottom re-examination of the formal State-DoD disaster assistance request process as it is supposed to work, as well as a review of the informal, back-channel process as it has tended to unfold.

This nexus of civilian government and military coordination across the full spectrum from development assistance planning to disaster relief missions reached a higher level of institutionalization as the U.S. government stood up a new unified combatant command for Africa (AFRICOM) in October 2008. For now, AFRICOM's primary focus will be on peacetime engagement with African partner countries as a way to help promote stability, build local security capabilities, and eradicate poor living conditions – such as the lack of clean water and food, inadequate health care, and limited educational facilities – that could breed civil unrest and possibly create opportunities for terrorist activities. In time, these cooperative security activities managed by AFRICOM should yield platforms for improving HA/DR readiness and operations.

AFRICOM's ability to move in this direction is helped by the fact that it began operations with an interagency- and CMCoord-based organizational structure designed from the start to encourage and support stability operations (of which HA/DR operations are an integral part) and civic aid missions (which generally improve local capabilities in the HA/DR realm). AFRICOM has a deputy commander for civil-military activities and a staff structure optimized in part for precisely these types of activities. When fully staffed, the command will have more civilians in key positions than any other command (GAO 2008, 9). Indeed, as one AFRICOM officer described it, "Our mission is 95 percent at least civil affairs," and military forces assigned to the command will spend much of their time drilling wells, building hospitals, training medics, and responding to local tragedies, such as a collapsed building in Kenya or a capsized ferry in Djibouti (Kristof 2007).

At least, that was the early vision. AFRICOM's first year has been a bumpy one, and the Government Accounting Office determined that the command "continues to face concerns from U.S. government, non-governmental, and African stakeholders about its mission and activities" (GAO 2009, 3). These concerns stem from a view by some that AFRICOM could "blur traditional boundaries between diplomacy, development, and defense." AFRICOM is aware of these worries and has been trying to adjust its mission statement and demonstrate sensitivity to the other stakeholders, but at some point the blurring of boundaries is actually part of the objective (at least to the extent that interagency teams operate more fluidly and effectively together).

One past example the command points to for inspiration was a "hearts and minds" mission in the Islamic Republic of Mauritania a few years ago, where a U.S. special forces team built a health clinic in coordination with the local ministry of defense. There were no local USAID officials to consult about the political and social context of the project, and the clinic ended up being built on military land restricted from public use. Now the clinic remains vacant and unused (Vandiver 2009).

The command has also experienced difficulty recruiting much of the non-military staff it planned to deploy, becoming "fully operational" in 2008 with only half of its expected DoD civilians and about a quarter of the interagency people assigned (GAO 2009, 3). In addition, efforts to find a home base for AFRICOM in Africa have been unsuccessful so far, and the command remains headquartered in Stuttgart, Germany. AFRICOM is making strides with military-to-military relations in the region, and it is assisting with training activities and disaster relief preparation and response efforts, which are relatively non-controversial. For all the costs involved in standing up a new command in the region, however, there will be many who will question the cost-effectiveness of these activities, especially if it takes money away from U.S. diplomatic or development aid initiatives in Africa.

Thus, despite the political wrangling over the respective roles and responsibilities of the departments of State and Defense, DoD has forged ahead with its planning efforts to prepare for the full spectrum of operations, including humanitarian assistance, disaster response, peace operations, stabilization and reconstruction, and war. In fact, the Joint Chiefs of Staff released a significant revision in March 2009 to its joint publication on foreign humanitarian assistance (Joint Publication 3-29), and Office of the Secretary of Defense for Policy (OSD/P) is in the midst of substantially updating DoD directive 5100.46, "Responsibilities for Foreign Disaster Relief Operations," a key DoD document last updated in 1975. Moreover, DoD has adjusted its procurement and training strategies to enhance its readiness for crisis response, including initiatives to improve CMCoord for humanitarian assistance and operations with NGOs and international organizations. Military planners are also developing a new vocabulary for HA/DR as opposed to combat operations, so that they can coordinate more seamlessly with their civilian counterparts.

Still, much remains to be done, and many U.S. officials see a need for continued efforts in this regard. The new assistant secretary of defense for Asian and Pacific affairs (former commanding general of the Marine Corps Forces Pacific, Chip Gregson) highlighted this in his confirmation process, noting that "Successful civilian-military collaboration reduces duplication of efforts, facilitates communication and information sharing, and increases the military's effectiveness" (Gregson 2009, 33). Enhancing CMCoord was the one example he gave when asked how to improve HA/DR efforts in the region.

Yet, DoD efforts to prepare for, and at times lead, disaster relief operations, have raised fears about the militarization of humanitarian aid. "The traditional distinction between the military and non-military domains of humanitarian aid is becoming obscure, and this is leading to a diminishing humanitarian space," commented one workshop participant. "The military should focus on areas where it has a comparative advantage, such as security, logistics, transport, and communications, rather than attempt to control the humanitarian response" (IFPA-OSIPP 2008).

Resistance to military involvement in disaster relief activities, however, is not about whether or not the military should participate in HA/DR operations, but about how best to integrate military and civilian assets to improve coordination. One NGO worker involved in the disaster response to the Pakistan earthquake criticized U.S. forces for taking on projects without consulting local relief workers. "We were grateful that the U.S. military delivered needed construction material, but we did not need them to also rebuild damaged infrastructure. By doing so, they were ignoring our efforts to engage the local populace in the recovery effort, build local capacity, and provide cash-for-work opportunities." Another workshop participant noted that military firewalls and classification policies also restricted the timely exchange of information, including weather forecasts.

Narrowing the cultural divide between civilian and military responders necessitates an increased understanding of the roles and resources of each actor involved in disaster relief, as well as their response to and assessment of a disaster situation. Military units are often referred to as the "sprinters," first to respond when assistance is requested and first to arrive with robust organizational and managerial skills, though they usually have a relatively short- or near-term perspective, such as "just getting the job at hand done." Military responders also tend to work hierarchically, to worry about force protection (which can inhibit the provision of assistance), and to prefer secure and controlled information flow (which might hamper CMCoord). On the other hand, civil humanitarian agencies, be they governmental offices or NGOs, are the "marathoners," slow to arrive in force, but able in time to bring to bear enormous depth of expertise, which they generally prefer to apply according to a long-term relief and recovery perspective. In so doing, they tend to prefer flat organizational structures, reaching decisions by consensus, open (non-secure) lines of communication, and a neutral, mediation-style approach to resolving conflicts.

These differences in culture, while not necessarily incompatible in a disaster relief situation, have often led to confusion and misconceptions as to what each community's best capabilities are, how quickly each can respond in an evolving operation, what the most effective division of labor between them might be over time, and what, at any point in time, either group is actually doing. Clearing away such confusion and correcting such misconceptions will be key to achieving a more rapid and effective response to future disasters and to encouraging a real unity of effort over the course of an operation. This will require, in turn, a more concerted effort to embed into practice civil-military lessons observed during past operations, but still not fully learned, if future operations are to go more smoothly. Indeed, thinking about and taking steps to maintain CMCoord across the lifecycle of an event – from first response to last act of assistance – remains central to the concept of continuous operations that is so vital to a well-managed relief effort, since it is the military sprinters who buy the time that the civilian marathoners need to fully mobilize and eventually assume command in the recovery and reconstruction phase of an HA/DR operation.

Of course, educational tools, expert meetings, and joint training and exercises should help create familiarity in the field and identify critical gaps in disaster response capabilities. To this end, the U.S. military has conducted numerous exercises to improve crisis response coordination and interaction with non-military actors, and USAID is looking to develop a joint training plan and course module with CMO officials on the foreign disaster relief decision process.

Finally, the NGO community also has attempted to increase collaboration with the military, while preserving their impartiality. InterAction (the American Council for Voluntary International Action), a coalition of over 160 U.S.-based international development and humanitarian NGOs, produced a DVD, Civil-Military Relations: Working with NGOs, to raise awareness of the working practices of NGOs. The Center for Excellence in Disaster Management and Humanitarian Assistance and U.S. PACOM subsequently produced a complementary DVD, Civil-Military Relations: Working with the Military. As these two DVDs demonstrate, striking the right balance between military and civilian relief workers during a disaster depends on greater interaction and planning before a disaster hits. "We need to think collectively about the core competencies of each actor to determine how best to coordinate our relief efforts and where to invest our resources," urged one workshop participant.

Japan

In Japan, MOFA does not have the physical equivalent of the State Department's crisis management center to coordinate a government operation, but it will often establish a JTF similar to that at the State Department when word of a disaster comes in from Japan's embassies, and it has

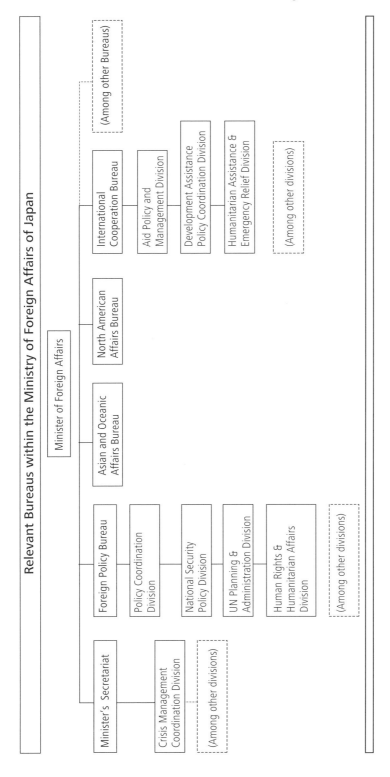

Relevant Bureaus within the Ministry of Foreign Affairs of Japan

Minister of Foreign Affairs

Minister's Secretariat
- Crisis Management Coordination Division
- (Among other divisions)

Foreign Policy Bureau
- Policy Coordination Division
- National Security Policy Division
- UN Planning & Administration Division
- Human Rights & Humanitarian Affairs Division
- (Among other divisions)

Asian and Oceanic Affairs Bureau

North American Affairs Bureau

International Cooperation Bureau
- Aid Policy and Management Division
- Development Assistance Policy Coordination Division
- Humanitarian Assistance & Emergency Relief Division
- (Among other divisions)

(Among other Bureaus)

steadily strengthened the ministry's crisis management capabilities.[40] In the case of the Indian Ocean tsunami, MOFA's task force was led by the relevant regional bureau, the Asian and Oceanian Affairs Bureau, but a key role was played by the Economic Cooperation Bureau, which managed Japan's overseas development and humanitarian assistance programs at that time. Another important player is Japan's International Cooperation Agency (JICA), which among other responsibilities serves as the secretariat for Japanese disaster relief teams frequently dispatched to assist overseas.

Recent reforms at MOFA have altered slightly the way that the ministry handles overseas development (and disaster) assistance (ODA). In 2006, MOFA changed the name of the Economic Cooperation Bureau to the International Cooperation Bureau and folded in certain components of MOFA's Global Issues Department. The Overseas Disaster Assistance Division (similar in some ways to OFDA in the United States) is situated within the International Cooperation Bureau. Also in 2006, the Japanese government established the Overseas Economic Cooperation Council to reinforce the ODA strategy formulation function of the Cabinet. The council is chaired by the prime minister and consists of the chief cabinet secretary, the minister of foreign affairs, the minister of finance, and the minister of economy, trade, and industry.

As part of this reform process, JICA merged with the overseas economic cooperation section of the Japan Bank for International Cooperation (JBIC) in October 2008 in order to better integrate the three schemes of Japan's overseas development assistance: 1) technical assistance (which was offered by the old JICA), 2) concessionary or ODA loans (formerly extended by JBIC), and 3) grant aid from MOFA (a substantial portion of which JICA administers). In addition, the new JICA established the JICA Research Institute to study past development programs and promote greater understanding of international development assistance mechanisms and programs. As a result of these organizational changes, JICA has emerged as one of the world's largest bilateral development

---

40   MOFA established the Crisis Management Coordination Division in 2005 (within the Management and Coordination Division of the Minister's Secretariat), which is meant to strengthen the foreign minister's oversight of MOFA's response. This followed the assignment of a deputy assistant vice-minister for crisis management within the Minister's Secretariat in 2004 (and this position was later promoted to assistant vice-minister for crisis management).

assistance agencies, with an estimated budget of $10.3 billion and over one hundred offices worldwide (JICA 2009).

Despite the reforms since 2006, Japan's response to the December 2004 tsunami is still a useful example of the basic way in which the government contributes to international disaster relief operations. Together with the Pakistan earthquake experience in 2005 and new challenges such as those in Iraq and Afghanistan, the tsunami experience taught Japan useful lessons that are informing future adjustments. In the wake of the tsunami, MOFA was the first in Japan to set up an emergency liaison office, on December 26, 2004. A day later the Cabinet Secretariat established a prime minister's liaison office, which was quickly upgraded to an emergency response headquarters. At an interagency meeting on January 4, 2005, however, it was decided that the foreign affairs section of the Cabinet Secretariat, rather than the Office for National Security and Crisis Management (which blends the MOD, MOFA, and the National Police Agency), would manage policy coordination for the relief operations. The Cabinet Secretariat helped to collect information from different ministries and agencies for the prime minister's office, but MOFA had its own channel to the prime minister, so the Secretariat's role was supplemental to MOFA's.

The Japan Defense Agency (JDA, before it became MOD in 2007) and the SDF quickly understood the scope of the U.S. military response to the tsunami disaster as it was being ramped up in Honolulu, since a Japanese liaison officer is permanently stationed at PACOM. The United States was seeking Japanese participation in the operation, and the JDA was keen to join. The JDA could immediately order three Maritime Self-Defense Force (MSDF) ships, which were in the region already, to assist with rescue operations, but it needed a request from the affected country to enable deployment within sovereign borders, and that required help from MOFA. In addition, the SDF could not be dispatched without a request to the JDA chief by the foreign minister, as per Japan's JDR Law.

MOFA, meanwhile, was initially focused on the health and safety of Japanese nationals affected by the tsunami, as opposed to the broader relief effort, so there was a brief period of disconnect before the Ground SDF on-call unit and other assets were mobilized. It did not help matters that the MOFA task force did not include personnel from the North

American Bureau or the National Security Division in the Foreign Policy Bureau, which are the two offices with the most frequent interaction with the JDA and maintain the strongest interpersonal contacts there. It did not take long, however, for the JDA to dispatch some of its own people into MOFA's Economic Cooperation Bureau for the duration of the operation. And overall, MOFA moved relatively quickly to engage the JDA. On December 28, Japan's foreign minister formally requested the SDF's assistance (via the JDA) for the relief effort, even if actual deployment took some additional time. The MOFA-MOD relationship should continue to strengthen as SDF dispatches in the region become more common,.

It is worth noting, however, that MOFA's Overseas Disaster Assistance Division does not have an office similar to the Office of Military Affairs or the Operational Liaison Unit at OFDA in the United States. MOFA might want to consider establishing such an office as the SDF increases its involvement in overseas disaster relief and peacekeeping missions. OMA plays an important role in fostering dialogue between civilian and military actors involved in U.S. relief missions, and it makes important contributions to the development of USAID's *Field Operations Guide for Disaster Assessment and Response*, among other policies. Moreover, OLU has the critical responsibility of bridging the gap between policy made in Washington and how it is carried out in the field (from "the suits to the boots," as one OFDA coordinator described it). To some extent, this is being managed now in Japan by the MOD's Joint Staff Office in collaboration with the divisions for policy and for training. But while this is improving MOD's and the SDF's interaction with international players such as OCHA and OFDA, it does not necessarily strengthen the MOFA-MOD connection. Seconding MOD personnel into a MOFA task force during an international crisis is a useful measure, but more regular interaction between the two organizations will be useful.

In recent years, MOFA's National Security Policy Division (within the Foreign Policy Bureau) has taken on more responsibility, and to some extent this demonstrates the degree to which Japan increasingly views global foreign policy issues through a national security lens. The International Peace Cooperation Division used to be housed in the UN Policy Division, for example, but in 2008 it was shifted into the National Security Policy Division. In addition to international peace cooperation, the National Security Policy Division is also home to the International-al Counter-Terrorism Cooperation Division and the Maritime Security Policy Division. The Ministry of Defense is also reforming itself to allow for more involvement by uniformed SDF officers in planning and policy development for overseas missions. Still, overall the relative power balance between MOFA and MOD on these types of issues is almost the opposite of that in the United States, with MOFA dominating policy planning and many operational aspects as well.

In part, this is because of Japan's legal and traditional restrictions on SDF funding and overseas operations, but it also underscores the primacy of diplomacy and foreign policy in Tokyo's geostrategic thinking. Japan is stepping up the SDF's involvement overseas in pursuit of diplomatic objectives, to support the U.S.-Japan alliance and to strengthen relations with other potential regional partners. This has manifested itself through more substantive Japan-Korea bilateral cooperation and in trilateral coordination with the United States. For example, Japan and South Korea signed a letter of intent in April 2009 to develop a cooperative defense and security relationship, with an early focus on non-traditional security cooperation including disaster relief and PKO missions (ROK Ministry of National Defense 2009). The three countries' defense communities established the Trilateral Steering Council in 2008 to cope better with transnational disasters and accidents (Kim 2008).

This trend can be seen in other regional bilateral and mini-lateral initiatives, such as Japan's diplomatic initiatives to strengthen security cooperation with Australia (Ministry of Foreign Affairs of Japan 2007) and India (Ministry of Foreign Affairs of Japan 2008a), and in each case disaster management, PKO, and humanitarian relief operations are key areas for cooperation. Moreover, the U.S.-Japan alliance is often able to become a de facto partner in these arrangements, and so there has been an increase in U.S.-Japan-Australia and U.S.-Japan-India joint exercises and exchanges in these areas. Japan, Korea, and China have agreed to similar initiatives, and all of these mini-lateral efforts help to support broader multilateral initiatives, such as a 2008 plan by ASEAN Regional Forum (ARF) countries to pool their military and civilian assets to respond to natural disasters (Joshi 2008). Multilateral framework agreements are useful, but usually it is the on-the-ground training and frequent interaction of consistent bilateral partners that contribute the most to improving coordination and developing lasting relationships.

To provide a sense of scale regarding some of the Japanese government's relief contributions, Japan responded to the 2004 tsunami by pledging $540 million, donating twenty thousand tons of rice, sending twelve medical and relief teams, and deploying its largest-ever disaster relief contingent. More than sixteen hundred SDF personnel were sent to the affected region, including three senior military officers (from the Joint Staff Office) tasked with helping to organize the aid effort on the ground. A C-130 cargo plane was also sent to Indonesia with forty SDF personnel to transport relief supplies. To coordinate with the U.S. military and other governments in the operation, Japan sent about twenty individuals to the regional operating headquarters at Utapao, Thailand. In response to the Pakistan earthquake, Japan provided about $20 million in emergency grant assistance and dispatched four SDF helicopters, two C-130 cargo planes, and over one hundred SDF personnel to help with relief deliveries, among other assistance. The government also followed up with a $100 million loan for recovery and rehabilitation efforts.

In response to cyclone Nargis in May 2008 in Myanmar, Japan sent $10 million in aid to fund a housing reconstruction project and $950 million in emergency relief supplies, including tents, blankets, plastic sheeting, sleeping mats, generators, and water purification equipment, most of which came from JICA's central warehouse in Singapore (Ministry of Foreign Affairs of Japan 2008b).[41] In fact, JICA maintains a permanent office in Myanmar to coordinate a series of technical and development assistance projects, such as assisting in the removal of sunken debris from the country's major port, studying means to improve the agricultural, health, and education sectors, and planning disaster prevention methods.

An important part of Japan's contributions to overseas disasters are its disaster relief teams, trained and managed by JICA and dispatched by MOFA's Overseas Disaster Assistance Division. These are pre-registered, volunteer civilian teams of medical and search-and-rescue professionals who are prepared to be dispatched anywhere in the world within forty-eight hours. JICA's disaster relief program divides the JDR teams into

---

41 JICA also maintains warehouses for pre-positioned relief supplies at Frankfurt in Germany, Johannesburg in South Africa, and Miami in the United States.

four types: 1) rescue teams, to search for missing people, rescue victims, and provide first aid; 2) medical teams; 3) expert teams, often including engineers or other specialists whose expertise corresponds to the type of disaster and who can assist with stopgap measures to help protect the population and speed recovery; and 4) SDF forces. As mentioned earlier, the SDF can not be dispatched without MOD approval.

Once a year, JICA organizes a drill for all JDR rescue teams, including personnel from MOFA, JICA, the National Police Agency, Fire Disaster Management Agency, and the Japan Coast Guard. The multi-day drill involves lectures for rescuers on various themes, basic rescue training, and a simulation of JDR team overseas deployment. Japanese JDR teams are strengthening their capabilities and endurance to earn the UN's "heavy" classification for relief teams, which will put them in the elite company of only seven other countries (including the United States and Great Britain) (*Yomiuri Shimbun* 2008a).

Within two days after the Pakistan earthquake, for example, MOFA dispatched a JDR rescue team consisting of forty-nine members (one from MOFA, fifteen from NPA, thirteen from FDMA, thirteen from the Coast Guard, three from JICA, two doctors, and two nurses). Eight days later that team returned, but it was followed by two medical teams of twenty-one members each (one from MOFA, five from JICA, four doctors, seven nurses, three paramedics, and one pharmacist). The Japanese Red Cross also sent its own medical relief team to Pakistan.

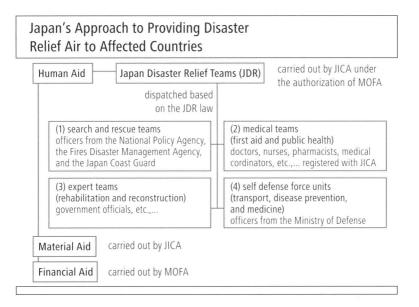

{ 85 }

In the wake of the Sichuan, China, earthquake in May 2008, JICA dispatched two JDR teams (sixty people total), which included specialists from the FDMA, the NPA, and the Coast Guard to assist with search-and-rescue efforts. Perhaps more significantly, this team was the first foreign assistance team China permitted to enter the country (Toy 2008). In addition, Japan sent a medical team (twenty-three people total), as well as large quantities of relief supplies, including seven hundred tents provided by JICA and one hundred supplied by the MOD and SDF (*People's Daily Online* 2008). JICA also provided blankets, plastic sheeting, sleeping mats, generators, water purification equipment, and water cans (JICA 2008).

In response to cyclone Nargis, JICA sent a medical team, which consisted of four doctors, seven nurses, one pharmacist, five medical coordinators, and five logistical coordinators, to Myanmar. When the medical team returned to Japan, it left behind equipment that could be used by other medical professionals still operating in the country (Ministry of Foreign Affairs of Japan 2008c). Over seven hundred medical volunteers are now registered with the JDR medical teams, along with close to two thousand search and rescue specialists. By including MOFA and JICA personnel in the JDR teams, those organizations get a hands-on perspective of local conditions which can be fed back to their headquarters in Tokyo as they plan for medium- and long-term recovery assistance.

The United States has similar teams in the area of search and rescue, though these are not assembled through individual volunteers and are instead existing emergency response units that have developed special partnerships with USAID and DHS. These units are also available to respond to domestic crises. Two examples are Virginia Task Force 1 from Fairfax County Fire and Rescue and a team from Los Angeles County Fire Department, which have deployed to disaster sites overseas as well as to assist after hurricane Katrina and the World Trade Center terrorist attacks in New York in 2001.

SDF involvement in international disaster relief operations will no doubt continue and will likely grow over time, not only because politicians and MOD want to see this happen, but also because the public increasingly approves of this trend. Cabinet office polls from 1991, 1998, and 2006 tested public support for the SDF's activities in international disaster relief, demonstrating a growth in support from about 54 percent in 1991 to over 90 percent in 2006. Opposition dropped from just over 30 percent to less than 6 percent (Yoshizaki 2006). As a result, MOD and the SDF have been rigorously studying CMCoord and CIMIC issues in the past few years. Two recent annual Tokyo Defense Forum conferences, for example, were focused exclusively on CMCoord and disaster relief operations.[42] The same was true for the Asia Pacific Security Seminar hosted in 2005 by Japan's National Institute for Defense Studies, as well as recent initiatives by Japan's Ground Self-Defense Forces (GSDF) as part of its so-called MCAP program (Multinational Cooperation in the Asia-Pacific region). There has been little discernable objection by the general public to the government's 2007 elevation of international peace cooperation activities to be a primary mission of the SDF.

Although there are many similarities between Japan and the United States with regard to motivations for expanding military involvement in disaster relief and peace-building operations, there are also some important differences. Both countries are responding to rising international expectations that wealthy nations will make appropriate military assets available when needed, and they both see opportunities to promote national interests by doing so. Japan tends to welcome these missions as an opportunity to enhance operational readiness, although restricted budgets and a shortage of sufficiently trained personnel often limit the country's response. The U.S. military, however, is stretched to the limit operationally and will only take on additional obligations when it is absolutely necessary.

For decades, for example, the U.S. Army has kept a brigade of the 82nd Airborne Division on constant alert to be able to respond to a cri-

---

42   The annual Tokyo Defense Forum involves military and defense officials from roughly two dozen countries (including Australia, Cambodia, Canada, China, India, Pakistan, Korea, Russia, the United States), as well as representatives from UN OCHA, the European Union, and the ASEAN Secretariat. A summary of the 11th Tokyo Defense Forum (October 2006) can be found at http://www.mod.go.jp/e/index_.htm.

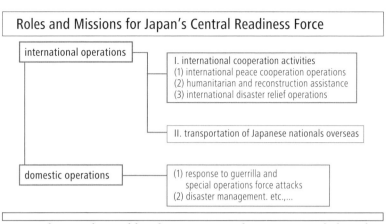

Roles and Missions for Japan's Central Readiness Force

international operations

I. international cooperation activities
(1) international peace cooperation operations
(2) humanitarian and reconstruction assistance
(3) international disaster relief operations

II. transportation of Japanese nationals overseas

domestic operations

(1) response to guerrilla and
special operations force attacks
(2) disaster management. etc.,...

sis anywhere in the world within one to two days. But extended combat deployments in Iraq and Afghanistan have forced the 82nd to begin transferring responsibility as a "division ready brigade" to the 101st airborne, which could lengthen its response time in certain situations (Price 2007). In contrast, Japan's SDF recently created the Central Readiness Force (CRF) (*chuo sokuo shudan*) as part of the GSDF. This new rapid reaction force, which formally stood up in March 2007, will be co-located with U.S. military personnel at Camp Zama in Japan by 2012, after new facilities are constructed to offer unique coordination opportunities.

The creation of the CRF grew out of Japan's National Defense Program Guideline for FY 2005 in order to better deal with multiple defense issues, ranging from large-scale disaster relief and humanitarian operations to international peacekeeping missions to counterterrorism and special operations. Today, the CRF is a "mixture of special forces, aerial transportation, anti-NBC (nuclear, biological, and chemical) warfare and military training units" (*DefenseNews* 2007). In all, the CRF consists of the 1st Airborne Brigade, the 1st Helicopter Brigade, the Central Readiness Force Regiment, the NBC Countermeasure Medical Unit, and the International Cooperation Activities Training and Education Unit, with personnel numbering over forty-two hundred (*DefenseNews* 2007).

As part of its functions as a rapid reaction force of the SDF, the CRF also strives to improve civil-military coordination in international operations. To this end, the CRF has held field seminars and exchanged views with U.S. and Australian forces, as well as civilian relief organizations, on planning for and conducting international peacekeeping and disaster relief operations. In June and August 2007, CRF units conducted several disaster prevention simulations with other SDF units in order to strengthen interoperability and improve the readiness and response of the JDR teams. Moreover, the CRF has participated in numerous international exercises, including Cobra Gold (a multilateral civil-military exercise), Khaan Quest (a multilateral peacekeeping exercise hosted by the U.S. and Mongolia), and the MCAP program (which the SDF has hosted annually since 2002). In addition, the International Cooperation Activities Training and Education Unit regularly hosts seminars, with U.S. military participation, on international activities, dispatch readiness, and lessons learned. Finally, the CRF has reached out to exchange information with numerous NGO partners, including Japan Platform, Peace Winds Japan, and the Japanese Red Cross Society, as well as several UN agencies such as OCHA, WFP, and UNDP.

Despite general political and MOD enthusiasm for SDF contributions abroad, as well as broad public approval, the trend is by no means without controversy, especially in the NGO community and to some extent within MOFA. Though SDF participation in disaster relief operations is less controversial than peacekeeping or peace-building missions, there is still concern that the inclusion of the SDF can diminish humanitarian space for aid workers and that it is rarely cost effective, thereby drawing

Structure of Japan Platform

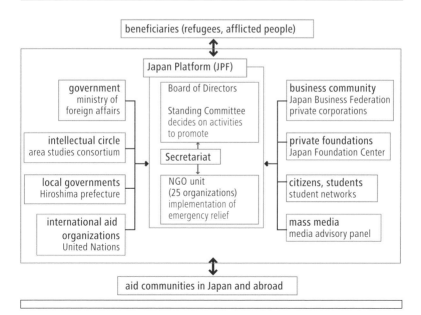

precious government resources away from struggling Japanese NGOs. Many of these NGOs recognize that the SDF can provide necessary capabilities and assets during certain emergencies, but even those NGOs considered to be "SDF friendly" would prefer that these contributions be kept to a minimum and restricted to infrastructure support or, in rare cases, indirect assistance.

The primary means by which Japanese NGOs participate in overseas disaster relief missions is through Japan Platform and its NGO unit, consisting of about thirty participating NGOs such as Peace Winds Japan, Japan Mine Action Service, the Japanese Red Cross Society, JEN, and Shanti Volunteer Association. Japan Platform began operations in 2001, largely at the instigation of MOFA; it provides emergency relief in natural disasters and refugee situations more quickly and efficiently than had previously been possible. It serves as a base from which NGOs can mobilize and carry out immediate relief activities, and it provides a way for these NGOs to pool resources for initial assessments at a disaster site and for operational and policy-oriented interaction with UN agencies and international organizations. Its activities are funded primarily through support from the government and to a smaller extent by contributions from corporations and individuals.

Japan Platform is the vanguard of Japan's disaster relief NGOs, with about fifteen members directly providing roughly $6 million in assistance following the Indian Ocean tsunami and at least eight members distributing $5 million worth of relief in the aftermath of the Pakistan earthquake. Japan Platform members have also provided assistance in Iran, Sudan, Liberia, Afghanistan, and Iraq, and they often have some of the best relationships with local NGOs in an affected region. Japan Platform's ability to organize collectively in close association with MOFA has been critical to improving its members' overall capabilities, in particular their capacity to respond quickly. This collective approach, however, also means that a consensus must be achieved among its members with regard to CMCoord and the SDF. As noted earlier, a number of Japanese NGOs are ideologically opposed to SDF involvement in missions overseas, whatever their configuration, and without the necessary consensus, the degree of direct dialogue between Japan Platform and the SDF is limited. This is problematic when one considers the limited financial and logistical strength that most Japanese NGOs possess, since some form of partnership with the SDF in terms of logistics and communications could be particularly helpful to Japanese civilian actors. The leadership at Japan Platform is trying to bridge this gap by working with MOFA, MOD, and the SDF to identify certain specific disaster relief scenarios that would be least controversial and that could benefit from closer coordination and cooperation.

To this end, Japan Platform organized a CMCoord study group to review existing guidelines and principles and exchange lessons learned from past operations with SDF personnel and other NGOs. In addition, Japan Platform organized a three-day workshop in 2008 with personnel from JICA, MOD, various international agencies, and the academic and NGO community to promote mutual understanding. During the workshop, participants discussed whether to create a set of CMCoord guidelines (in line with existing OCHA guidelines) for Japanese NGO and SDF use, as well as whether to create a website to improve information sharing between military and civilian relief partners. Other possible initiatives identified at the workshop include sharing contact lists, mapping the response capacities of the Japanese NGO community, improving relations with UN agencies and the international NGO community, and conducting a civil-military simulation exercise. Unfortunately, since many Japanese NGOs oppose any dialogue with SDF units, it is unlikely that many of the workshop's proposals will materialize any time soon. That said, frequent and increased dialogue between Japan Platform and the SDF may over time lessen NGO opposition and improve civil-military cooperation.

Japanese NGOs can also strengthen relations with the broader international NGO community. Relative to other countries, particularly the United States, Japanese NGOs lack experience, and joint training and exchange programs would help close this gap. For example, Peace Winds Japan has collaborated with Mercy Corps, and the two organizations work together in Iraq and regularly exchange officers. Moreover, such partnerships grant Japanese NGOs greater access to superior financial and material resources. For instance, Peace Winds Japan's budget for 2007 was $10 million, whereas Mercy Corps U.S. had over $186 million in total revenue for 2007 (Mercy Corps 2007a).[43] Clearly, any collab-

---

43   Figures for Mercy Corps US only.

oration between the two organizations pays significant dividends for Peace Winds Japan.

Of course, U.S.-based NGOs also benefit from collaborating with Japanese NGOs. On this point, one participant at the 2008 IFPA-OSIPP workshop asked, "What, if any, incentives does a U.S.-based NGO have to collaborate with a Japanese NGO?" In short, as discussed at the workshop, Japanese NGOs can serve as a staff and knowledge multiplier for U.S.-based NGOs. First, U.S.-based NGOs have an abundance of resources, but are often short on staff. Depending on the operation, U.S.-based NGOs face higher security threats that prevent them from carrying out their mission. For instance, when most NGOs and UN agencies were pulling out of Afghanistan as the security environment deteriorated, Peace Winds Japan and JEN continued to operate in the country without much resistance because Japan is not a member of NATO. This was also the case when NATO began its bombing campaign during the 1999 conflict in Kosovo.

Second, U.S.-based NGOs are sometimes unable to gain immediate access to certain countries (unless a presence already exists on the ground). In response to cyclone Nargis, for example, AAR Japan, which has a long history of working in Myanmar, was able to assist with relief efforts almost immediately. Third, NGOs based in the United States and Europe lack the capacity to respond to every situation across the globe. A partnership with Japanese NGOs would alleviate such pressures if loose burden-sharing agreements could be worked out.

Finally, no single NGO has the capacity to handle all aspects of a HA/DR operation. American and Japanese NGOs could look to develop complementary projects and capabilities over the long term. For instance, a Japanese NGO conducting a water and sanitation project in a disaster-stricken country would reinforce the activities of an American NGO working on health-related issues. Of course, this will only work well if the two governments are in synch overall with their development programs and working constructively with other nations and international organizations.

Promoting Bilateral Cooperation within International Frameworks

In response to the Indian Ocean tsunami, thirty-five countries contributed military assets and deployed more than thirty thousand personnel to disaster-affected areas (IFPA-OSIPP 2006). In 2005, about nineteen countries sent military equipment and soldiers into Pakistan following the South Asia earthquake (Center for Excellence in Disaster Management and Humanitarian Assistance 2006). In 2008, dozens of countries, international aid organizations, and private companies also donated funds and services totaling over $300 million to assist relief and recovery efforts in response to the earthquake in China (ReliefWeb 2008). In all cases, the UN and its affiliated agencies and organizations, along with countless NGOs, international organizations, private-sector companies, and government agencies provided valuable support and relief.

The huge scale and impromptu nature of these types of operations mean that no amount of centralized planning or organizational bureaucracy will be able to manage an initial response as a single coherent and cohesive mission. Still, incremental improvements can be made each year if the most influential contributors (such as the United States, Japan, the UN, and a few others) can agree on a set of CMCoord and related priorities for joint action. Moreover, by taking steps in this area, the United States and Japan can improve their alliance interoperability and increase the value that the alliance provides to the two nations' citizens and to others around the world.

As noted throughout this report, civilian and military planners worldwide are exploring various means to improve crisis response coordination, such as introducing revised national response plans and drafting new military protocols to address HA/DR activities. Despite sincere efforts to enhance disaster preparedness planning and response, much work remains to be done, and relatively few attempts have been made to connect all actors involved in HA/DR activities in concrete policy discussions. In fact, in some cases even national government agencies and militaries are reevaluating policies for crisis response without sufficiently coordinating their efforts with one another, let alone with other nations, the UN, NGOs, and the private sector.

Addressing disaster management issues without engaging all parties involved in relief operations, however, only leads to ineffective reform and poorly coordinated action on the ground. The inadequate response to hurricane Katrina illustrates this point. After the September 11 terrorist attacks, the U.S. government introduced a new emergency response system that did not sufficiently involve DoD and representatives from the NGO and private-sector communities in the planning process. As a result, the response to the hurricane was beset with communication problems, inaccurate damage assessments, and poor coordination among local, federal, and military actors. "If disaster preparedness planning and training is not inclusive, we will continue to face coordination challenges on the ground regardless of the policy changes in place," warned one workshop participant (IFPA-OSIPP 2006).

Effective interagency and civil-military coordination is crucial for gaining situational awareness, assessing needs, matching supply and demand, sharing assets and capabilities, and providing timely relief during a crisis. Joint planning and exercises between civilian and military actors in either a domestic, bilateral, or multilateral framework can greatly enhance the capacity for domestic and international humanitarian and disaster response. As mentioned earlier, the relative success of the response to the Indian Ocean tsunami was in many ways a result of the joint training done earlier at the annual, multilateral Cobra Gold exercise in Thailand.

Another valuable multilateral initiative is the Multinational Planning Augmentation Team (MPAT), which works to improve crisis response and force interoperability in the Asia-Pacific region through a series of workshops and seminars among the thirty-three member states and several UN, international, and nongovernmental agencies, such as the WHO,

Doctors Without Borders, the International Committee of the Red Cross, and OCHA. An MPAT workshop in summer 2007 focused on responding to a pandemic flu outbreak in the region, and it involved a wide range of military and civilian actors. More recently, MPAT nations conducted a Tempest Express workshop in Manila from March 26-April 3, 2009, to focus on disaster relief procedures. Twenty-four nations sent ninety-three military personnel, and humanitarian participation consisted of representatives from OCHA, WFP, and the International Federation of the Red Cross (PACOM 2009). In December 2009, MPAT plans to host a Southeast Asia disaster management workshop in Indonesia.

Though multinational exercises allow participants to develop standard operating procedures and enhance nation-to-nation cooperation, they are difficult to coordinate, time consuming, and costly. They become less focused as the number of partners increases. That is, in order to meet all participants' training priorities and political objectives (or avoid political sensitivities), the exercises can get watered down and fail to address in sufficient detail certain key issues common to disaster relief operations, such as public safety and security, information exchange, and medical assistance. Outside of OCHA, CMCoord does not really have an institutional champion to promote its training priorities, and since OCHA is not normally a lead player in these types of exercises, CMCoord issues are often inadequately addressed.

As a result, CMCoord mechanisms are tested rarely, especially as the number of non-military participants present at these exercises remains low. "We don't have the budget or staff to attend all training programs," explained one NGO representative at the 2006 IFPA-OSIPP workshop. Moreover, concerns over the potential militarization of humanitarian aid also have kept some relief agencies away from exercises or seminars that involve military personnel. "In Japan, NGOs hesitate to work or even train alongside the military, fearing it will impact their ability to operate with impartiality and independence," added another workshop participant, who went on to explain how difficult it was to receive authorization even to attend the workshop (IFPA-OSIPP 2006).

Nevertheless, NGOs continue to participate in exercises and workshops whenever possible. At the 2008 IFPA-OSIPP workshop in Tokyo, the number of NGO representatives (and participating organizations) had more than doubled from the previous workshop. NGOs, however, remain cautious when working alongside military personnel in the field. "NGOs are not anti-military. NGOs recognize the invaluable role that the military plays in a disaster relief operation," explained one NGO representative. "But the proliferation of military actors in HA/DR missions has threatened the security and perceived impartiality of the NGO community. It is for this reason that military partners should stop referring to NGOs as 'force multipliers'" (IFPA-OSIPP 2008). NGO staff is also frustrated when the military refers to some of its own work as "humanitarian," since the term describes (among other attributes) a level of impartiality that is practically impossible for a military organization to provide.

Since it is difficult for NGOs to maintain close ties to military personnel in the field, it becomes even more imperative that coordination begins before a disaster strikes. Indeed, even if NGO and military personnel do not physically work together in the field, there are numerous opportunities to coordinate response efforts away from the disaster zone. One participant at the 2008 workshop explained that during the tsunami response an NGO had difficulty receiving authorization to load emergency relief supplies onto an American C-130. In the end, it was a matter of simple paperwork. At a minimum, joint exercises and periodic meetings can help establish appropriate points of contact. "If all I get out of a meeting or exercise is a bunch of business cards, that is enough. I will know whom to call when I am out in the field" (IFPA-OSIPP 2008).

Of course, not all NGOs are against working alongside the military in the field. In fact, many NGOs welcome opportunities, particularly in response to large-scale disasters, to work with foreign militaries given their unique resources and reach. "True, NGOs and militaries do not agree on everything, but rather than focus on one another's cultural differences and other points of contention, we should focus on areas of agreement," recommended one 2008 IFPA-OSIPP workshop participant.

Indeed, periodic exercises, workshops, and expert meetings within a bilateral framework may enable more candid, constructive dialogue between civil and military planners, as long as the framework reinforces the efforts of OCHA and regional organizations. Close allies are better able to tackle sensitive issues such as mutual support and assistance agreements, security and customs clearances, aircraft use and landing authorizations, and shared information and communication networks.

During hurricane Mitch in 1998, for example, Japan's Air SDF (ASDF) operated a significant airlift operation to Honduras involving six C-130 transports and over one hundred ASDF personnel out of Kelly Air Force Base near San Antonio, Texas.

In addition, with fewer countries and training priorities to compete with, civil and military planners can better take on field coordination issues, harmonize operating procedures, and achieve greater mutual awareness and understanding. "At minimum, countries should improve bilateral efforts within a specific region," recommended one 2008 workshop participant. In fact, in March 2009, senior defense officials from Japan and the ten member countries of ASEAN met to discuss nontraditional security issues facing the Asia-Pacific region, including disaster mitigation. The United States and Japan too can make important contributions in this regard, and alliance managers have been working to enhance the bilateral security relationship on this front.

Since 2002, the United States and Japan have held a series of working- and high-level consultations to clarify their common strategic objectives and outline steps to transform and strengthen the alliance. Pursuant to these discussions, the two countries made important commitments regarding force posture realignment and the delineation of shared and complementary roles and missions. These commitments were outlined in October 2005 by the U.S.-Japan Security Consultative Committee (SCC), also known as a "2+2" meeting since it consisted of the cabinet-level leadership for defense and foreign affairs in both countries.

That SCC document, "U.S.-Japan Alliance: Transformation and Realignment for the Future," identified key areas for alliance improvement such as air defense, counter-proliferation, search and rescue, humanitarian relief, reconstruction assistance, and non-combatant evacuation operations. Specifically, the document emphasized close and continuous bilateral policy coordination at every level of government, enhancing information sharing, and intelligence cooperation among related ministries and agencies, developing common operational procedures, and conducting regular military exercises, including with third parties. A follow-up 2+2 meeting in 2007 noted some progress in these areas, including the signing of a general security of military information agreement (GSOMIA) to further facilitate information sharing, along with the establishment of a bilateral CBRN (chemical, biological, radiological, and nuclear) defense working group that fosters interagency coordination and addresses consequence management issues. The statement also noted the creation of a "flexible, bilateral coordination mechanism to coordinate policy, operational, intelligence, and public affairs positions before and during crisis situations" (U.S.-Japan Security Consultative Committee 2007).

In the area of working with other nations, there has also been progress, as indicated earlier with the expansion of bilateral and mini-lateral security cooperation initiatives. For example, the United States, Japan, and Australia are working together on airlift cooperation applicable to disaster relief missions. Since Japan has limited transportation options and Australia has limited rotary-wing assets, American and Australian airmen worked with Japan GSDF members in February 2009 to load a Japanese CH-47J Chinook, which is slightly larger than an American CH-47, into a C-17 Globemaster III at Yokota Air Base. During the tsunami relief efforts, Japan lacked the strategic airlift to move its fleet of CH-47Js into the disaster zone, and there was not enough time to coordinate moving the helicopters using foreign fixed-wing aircraft. Japan faced the same problem in response to the Pakistan earthquake. Instead, Japan moved the helicopters via ship, which took approximately 10 days. The ability to load a CH-47J onto a C-17 improves the ability of the United States, Japan, and Australia to compensate for the gaps in one another's resources and coordinate a rapid respond to a crisis. In addition, the United States, Japan, and India announced plans to conduct joint naval exercises in 2009 focused on the necessary safety measures to be taken in the event of a large-scale natural disaster in the Pacific.

With regard to civil-military coordination, the 2005 SCC document proposed the dual civil-military use of USFJ facilities in Japan to meet local emergency needs during disasters and other crises, as well as for commercial use. At a subsequent 2+2 meeting in May 2006, the two countries agreed to study the specific conditions for possible dual-use strategies over the course of twelve months, but progress has been slow and the effort remains controversial. In 2006, for example, the Aomori prefectural government twice rejected U.S. requests to use a civilian airport for protocol visits and to supply a nearby radar site (*Asahi Shimbun* 2007). In late 2008, the issue was still on the bilateral agenda (*Yomiuri Shimbun* 2008b).

This is an important opportunity for two main reasons. First, dual use and co-location increase opportunities to enhance CMCoord. In just one example, during the initial stages of the hurricane Mitch operation, nearly all commercial flights to the disaster area out of Miami International Airport were canceled because of bad weather, but across the airfield U.S. military flights operated under fewer restrictions and were able to take off. This allowed some of the initial civilian assessment and relief teams that were waiting at the airport to reach disaster sites more quickly. Second, to the extent that dual use can deliver added value to local communities in Japan (either through a quicker response in times of crisis or just through greater access to high-quality facilities in normal times), then USFJ realignment and alliance transformation should enjoy that much more political and public support (interview 2007a).

The findings of our project suggest to us that it is probably too difficult (and unnecessary) to try to bridge the gaps between the military and civilian sectors for disaster relief situations in a comprehensive way. In other words, U.S.-Japan military-to-military interactions and parallel civilian-to-civilian interactions are likely to be much more productive than trying to integrate civil-military dialogues and policies *across the alliance* with any sort of regularity.

Of course, these parallel civilian and military interactions need to be connected to each other in some way in order to set complementary goals and maintain communication and mutual awareness as they progress, but it is not necessary to impose common CMCoord solutions on the alliance. In this sense, American CMCoord and Japanese CMCoord will be like two different doors that open with their own key, but there should be a master key that can work both doors when the need arises. Developing this link between the two, in conjunction with the UN and other partners in the region, is a significant challenge for all major contributors to international disaster relief missions.

Overall, this linkage and these interactions should focus most on planning, preparation, communication, and assessment issues related to disaster relief, since actual operations are more likely to be carried out separately by U.S. and Japanese forces and civilian teams. Promoting joint U.S.-Japan disaster relief operations, therefore, does not need to be a specific goal of alliance managers, but more efficient and productive coordination of U.S. and Japanese contributions to these multinational operations is a worthwhile objective. This can start at the far end of the preparation and planning spectrum, including coordinated disaster reduction and management capacity building through development assistance to disaster-prone countries, as well as adjusting (or perhaps adding to) pre-positioned stockpiles of disaster relief supplies throughout the region.

Bilateral cooperation in this area can also move into more detailed planning tasks by identifying complementary specialties or a viable division of labor in certain circumstances, standardizing information flows (such as scripting requests for assistance and collaborating on advance contracting arrangements), and harmonizing damage- and needs-assessment procedures. The fact that there is an explicit commitment to strengthening security cooperation overall provides a useful framework for addressing disaster relief scenarios and CMCoord issues.

Periodic tabletop exercises and expert meetings on disaster relief operations can help to identify the gaps and opportunities for enhanced U.S.-Japan cooperation. Given the expected role of U.S. and Japanese military forces in disaster relief missions, military-to-military exercises and consultations are essential to identifying the capacities of each country; they also help to standardize operating procedures, planning efforts, and communication and information-sharing networks. Moreover, more frequent military-to-military consultations help identify significant challenges, such as legal frameworks that may inhibit cooperation or the absence of agreements that address cost issues related to the dual use of assets or the provision of fuel. The next challenge for the allies is to expand and integrate their joint exercises and training with other partners in the region, despite the logistical challenges this poses.

As one former high-ranking U.S. military officer put it, "The United States cannot be an 'Asian nation' or a major player in Asia without allies...and...generals and admirals sipping tea can take security cooperation only so far. One must have forces [in the region] to train with the forces of other nations so that our young people can validate the grand pronouncements of us senior officers" (interview 2004). Increasingly this kind of so-called theater security cooperation (TSC) involves more than just two allies working together, in part because the number of capable and willing partners in Asia has grown in recent years (as such countries as India, Thailand, and others become wealthier and better equipped). Shared interests in regional stability, open trade, anti-piracy and counter-terrorism, disaster relief, and similar objectives are prompting more frequent collaboration. These joint exercises can include, it is worth noting, the construction of warehouses, supply depots, airstrips, and port facilities (as a part of "exercise-related construction") to which the allies might be granted access during future contingencies.

The budgets supporting TSC and related training activities are relatively modest, however, and annual requests within the commands are often twice what is available. "Unfortunately, TSC is often perceived as competition for 'real' needs," commented a U.S. officer. "But TSC is not just something we do for our partners... it is a vital part of training our forces...in the art of conducting military operations in the difficult environment of coalition politics. At the tactical and operational level, knowing how to work with forces from different cultural backgrounds and different doctrinal schools is exceedingly important and tough to learn from a book" (interview 2004). As we look to expand TSC activities in the HA/DR area, however, we should keep in mind the AFRICOM example of an abandoned medical clinic mentioned earlier. The value of these investments can be greatly enhanced through more effective and timely coordination between the military and civilian officials and specialists.

Predominately civilian interactions should be fostered as well, and an element of cross-fertilization with the military must be incorporated. This has been happening more frequently in recent years, but it should continue with regularity. Joint training exercises may lead to some degree of specialization or division of labor between U.S. and Japanese forces and civilian actors, as well as with those from other countries. These bilateral activities can be expanded in certain situations to include third countries, as noted above, concentrating on more traditional partners such as Australia and South Korea, but also including new partners such as India, Russia, and possibly even China at some point. In fact, Japan, South Korea, and China met in December 2008 to discuss enhanced cooperation in disaster relief, including disaster mitigation, information-strengthening, and the development of a comprehensive disaster management framework. The three countries agreed to hold in turn trilateral meetings with the heads of their respective disaster response agencies.

Another step in improving the ability of the United States and Japan to effectively pool their civilian and military resources in response to humanitarian crises is to identify and catalogue what assets (civil and military personnel, material and equipment, and support assets) are available to each country for HA/DR activities, particularly in Asia. This process should help familiarize U.S. and Japanese officials with one another's capacities to respond to a crisis, without necessarily committing either party to exchange logistics support and services. This exercise could also go beyond pinpointing available military assets, such as heavy-lift helicopters, naval vessels, and surveillance equipment, to also identify private-sector and NGO capabilities. Private-sector capabilities are particularly well suited to the areas of communication, damage assessment (involving commercial satellites and local NGO staff), and transportation.

Understanding the roles and resources of each actor involved in disaster relief creates familiarity at the strategic and operational levels of a mission, as well as helping to identify critical gaps in each country's disaster response capacities. In time, this process may lead to the development of a disaster management database, similar to OCHA's Central Register of Disaster Management Capacities. A bilateral inventory list specifying the civilian and military assets, support services, and personnel available for or, at minimum, trained for complex emergencies could enhance the capacity of the United States and of Japan to respond, either alone or together, to an emerging crisis. Exchanging information on the availability of military assets would also help U.S. and Japanese planning efforts.

But a bilateral effort in this area should be well coordinated with OCHA and other regional efforts, such as the contact points for the disaster relief database compiled by the ARF. Databases such as these are notorious for becoming quickly outdated and inaccurate. An internet search for the ARF contact list, for example, yields two different versions.[44] The more recent (and presumably more accurate) version identifies for Japan MOFA's National Security Policy Division as a contact point, but while this division does generally handle ARF matters,

---

44   One list can be found at http://www.aseansec.org/17069.htm, and a similar (but different) list is at http://www.aseanregionalforum.org/Contacts/ARFContact-PointsforDisasterRelief/tabid/137/Default.aspx.

it is not directly involved in disaster relief issues. There is significant room to improve database development and management, and this could be a productive area for enhancing efficiency through bilateral cooperation within multilateral frameworks. Data formats and terms of reference should be consistent.

Including database information on NGO and private-sector companies might also enable government officials to share the response burden and delegate responsibilities to those more experienced or equipped to handle certain crisis situations. Indeed, many local and international NGOs were working in Pakistan long before the earthquake hit. For example, Mercy Corps, a humanitarian organization that provides relief and development assistance worldwide, has been working in Pakistan since 1985, and it had over 180 staff in the country prior to the earthquake (Mercy Corps 2007b). Like Mercy Corps, local and international NGOs are embedded in local society. They are familiar with local customs and are better able to determine the short- and long-term needs of the local community than the foreign militaries are, particularly with regard to gender issues, nutrition assistance, and recovery efforts. Here might be an opportunity for Japan and the United States each to work with its own NGOs to enhance their ability to tap into these local networks, and then to develop a mechanism for sharing information in an appropriate manner. Moreover, the two allies should foster bilateral ties between their NGO communities. Japan and Taiwan recently launched an international disaster relief and rescue platform to coordinate the humanitarian aid efforts of NGOs in the Southeast Asia region. Under the leadership of Japan and Taiwan, a MOU was signed by nine NGOs from Taiwan, six from Japan, and one each from the United States and Indonesia at the Southeast Asian NGO Forum in April 2009 (*China Post* 2009). As part of the agreement, the signatory NGOs will work to create a mechanism within four years to coordinate their humanitarian aid efforts for HA/DR missions.

The private sector remains another relatively untapped resource despite its increasing role in recent disaster relief efforts. In addition to making substantial financial contributions, the private sector can supply operational support across several functional areas, including transport, logistics, and communications. Digital Globe, a U.S.-based earth-imaging and information company, provided satellite imagery to disaster officials and local aid workers in Indonesia following the tsunami to help determine where to build refugee camps, medical facilities, communication networks, and transportation routes (DigitalGlobe 2005a). The company offered similar assistance to officials in New Orleans following hurricane Katrina. Digital Globe's satellite imagery showed officials the extent of the flooding and the locations of levee breaks (DigitalGlobe 2005b). Moreover, the company launched an online clearinghouse of satellite images for officials, relief workers, and private citizens to access (DigitalGlobe 2005a).

There is also a for-profit dimension where companies can be successful by designing and adapting emerging technologies to address key challenges faced by relief workers, governments, international organizations, and the military. Global Relief Technologies, for example, has developed the Rapid Data Management System, which uses hand-held remote devices uplinked to a central database as a means to gather information about an unfolding disaster and facilitate distribution of that information to other users on the network. The handheld devices can be tracked by GPS, and field workers can use them to take photos, scan barcodes, and instantly update data to a user account. Regardless of the language the field worker interface uses (Japanese, Korean, or English), the data fields are consistent and can be shared easily throughout the network (IFPA-OSIPP 2008). The American Red Cross has already begun deploying this technology to conduct damage assessments in the United States.

The Japanese business community has also provided valuable support in times of crisis. In collaboration with Japan Platform, Nippon Yusen Kaisha, a shipping company, delivered containers loaded with such aid supplies as power generators, blankets, and rice from Taiwan and Japan to ports near earthquake-stricken areas in Pakistan from October 2005 to June 2006 (Nippon Yusen Kaisha 2006). Several Japanese companies made financial contributions to past disaster relief efforts as well, including Toshiba and Hitachi Global. Directly managing private-sector cooperation and contributions is probably not the proper role for the U.S. or Japanese government, but they can perhaps encourage a bilateral dialogue through the respective chambers of commerce in each country by way of seminars or even working groups that include some government and UN officials.

Promoting a comprehensive civilian-to-civilian bilateral dialogue on these issues will be difficult and unwieldy, which is why sector-specific forums might prove the most productive. On this point, one participant at the 2008 IFPA-OSIPP workshop remarked, "In the United States, policy makers, military officials, and aid workers are ready to talk about CMCoord, but this is not the case in Japan. To begin with, the *civil* side of the civil-military equation is not coordinated. Partnerships between NGOs, the private sector, and the government do not exist. Increased interaction with U.S. NGO and private-sector representatives should help Japan establish networks similar to those in the United States, such as InterAction, the National Voluntary Organizations Active in Disaster, and Disaster Resource Network." In fact, all three of these organizations are actively pursuing professional partnerships in Japan, although this can be time consuming and requires some financial commitment to sustain. A wide variety of networks can be tapped to foster this civilian-to-civilian dialogue, including chambers of commerce and even sister city relationships (some of which span more than five decades and go beyond art and cultural exchanges to include various civil society organizations and local governments).

Another means to improve government and military relations with NGOs and the private sector, as well as enhance U.S.-Japan cooperation overall, is the establishment of mutual assistance and support agreements, or MOUs, for disaster relief operations. As mentioned earlier, the current U.S.-Japan Acquisition and Cross-Servicing Agreement enables U.S. and Japanese forces to provide mutual logistics support, exchange supplies--including food and fuel--and use each other's transportation and communications equipment, for reimbursement either in cash, replacement in kind, or equal value exchange. But the potential applicability of this agreement is not well understood in the broader disaster relief community, and although it can be invoked in disaster relief situations, it is not specifically designed to do so. "Plans need to be made and agreed upon. We need to assess ahead of time what is needed, when will it be needed, and who will provide it," urged one 2008 workshop participant. Developing basic scripted RFAs or MOUs tailored to general disaster relief scenarios might be useful in this regard.

In addition to military-to-military MOUs, the two countries might study the benefits of signing MOUs with humanitarian and private sector organizations. UN agencies, for example, have signed MOUs with several NGO and private-sector organizations, such as the International Federation of the Red Cross and Red Crescent Societies, OXFAM GB, and Deutsche Post World Net, the parent company of DHL, an international express and logistics company. Under the UN-DHL disaster management partnership, DHL has agreed to set up disaster response teams in Asia, the Middle East, and Latin America. In April 2006, the company fielded its first disaster response team in Singapore. In the event of a crisis, specially trained DHL employees will help manage logistics operations in airports close to disaster-affected regions. Though DHL did not formalize its relations with the UN until late 2005, the company had already participated in several disaster relief missions. DHL provided airport freight handling and assistance to international relief teams in Sri Lanka following the tsunami and in Iran and Pakistan following major earthquakes in 2003 and 2005, respectively.

Standby arrangements for disaster management and emergency response between U.S. and Japanese civil and military partners would also enhance the ability of the two countries to mobilize resources quickly. A standby arrangement would commit each party to maintain specified resources on standby, such as technical and logistics resources, field staff, and material and equipment. Joint capacity-mapping exercises could help identify the allies' strengths and weaknesses, reveal which areas require additional investment, in terms of resources, personnel, and training, as well as determine which assets U.S. and Japanese forces should make available to one another to avoid duplications in assistance efforts. Moreover, this process could identify how best to integrate the UN, NGOs, and private-sector companies into disaster preparedness plans and relief efforts.

For now, standby arrangements for military capabilities might be difficult to implement, but introducing bilateral standby arrangements between U.S. and Japanese government agencies, NGOs, and private-sector companies could be more feasible. For some time, OCHA has had in place standby arrangements with governments and humanitarian organizations for the provision of emergency staff and equipment during disasters. The UN Department of Peacekeeping has in place a similar arrangement, the UN Stand-by Arrangement System (UNSAS). Furthermore, in the wake of the Indian Ocean tsunami, the ARF proposed establishing similar arrangements for regional disaster response and humanitarian activities. The degree of U.S. and Japanese involvement in these programs, however, has been limited, and neither is well aware of the other's national agreements, such as they are. The two countries could consider comparing and, when appropriate, further developing bilateral standby arrangements with relief agencies and commercial aircraft carriers and shipping companies, for example, with an eye toward establishing some element of reciprocity with each other and perhaps with other nations and organizations.

Information management is an overriding challenge for CMCoord, though this seemingly simple objective can mean slightly different things to different stakeholders. For many at OCHA, greater standardization of how information is provided by and managed among crisis response partners is the top priority for improving CMCoord (interview 2006b). From their perspective, this includes information about the availability and capability of certain assets or personnel, the terms for their deployment, standardization of assessment reports and procedures, and a high degree of interoperability among the contributing organizations and governments.

For some this is a process of developing compatible systems, but others might emphasize the development of compatible people (people trained to understand how different responding organizations operate and what they can offer) (interview 2006c). "At minimum, it is essential to share common training techniques to ensure that international guidelines and best practices are learned," recommended one participant at the 2008 IFPA-OSIPP workshop. Still others take this a step further and emphasize the personal relationships among responders in the field as the key factor (interview 2007b). "At the end of the day, having a strong working relationship with representatives from various organizations helps mitigate coordination issues in the field," added another participant. All of these perspectives are valid, but each of them suggests a slightly different focus for CMCoord training and cooperation in a bilateral (or mini-lateral) context. Developing practical options to increase and strengthen U.S.-Japan peer-to-peer interactions on CMCoord issues, while maintaining connections between these groups, should help the two countries to clarify how they can best contribute to the process of CMCoord improvement.

Overall, strengthening the U.S.-Japan alliance for disaster response may increase the two countries' participation in regional and multilateral HA/DR missions, which will be a good thing for affected nations and for the alliance. Harmonizing policies and procedures among close allies would improve how they cooperate together or as members of a coalition, as well as pave the way for achieving a more efficient international framework for disaster response and recovery. Finally, opportunities for enhanced U.S.-Japan civil-military cooperation in disaster management and emergency response can serve as a catalyst for greater cooperation throughout the Asia-Pacific region for missions such as peacekeeping, counterproliferation, counterterrorism, and maritime security. The first step, however, is to continue improving U.S.-Japan CMCoord in times of crisis.

References

ActionAid International. 2006. *The evolving UN cluster approach in the aftermath of the Pakistan earthquake: An NGO perspective.* http://www.actionaid.org/docs/un_cluster_approach.pdf.

American Red Cross. 2008. *2008 annual report.* For the fiscal year ending June 30, 2008. http://www.redcross.org/www-files/Documents/pdf/corppubs/A501-08.pdf

Asahi Shimbun. 2007. Aomori rejects 2 U.S. military requests to use civilian airport. February 5.

Asia Press Network. 2004. Report on the situation for the SDF in Iraq. December 28. http://www.asiapressnetwork.com/depths/library/20041228_01_01.html [in Japanese].

Bennett, John. 2009. Flournoy: Create a U.S. civilian response corps. *DefenseNews*, March 30.

Braithwaite, Kenneth. 2007. U.S. humanitarian assistance/disaster relief: Keys to success in Pakistan. *Joint Force Quarterly*, issue 44 (1st quarter 2007).

Business Civic Leadership Center. 2005. From relief to recovery: The 2005 U.S. business response to the Southeast Asia tsunami and Gulf Coast hurricanes. http://www.uschamber.com/NR/rdonlyres/ecphnbd7xgk7updusn6ebb3zdjkdomwifbcyro5jfqsg2nuivb2tezm7uddzrls3gzgdzkzffgdxwperbmy7uolwxie/from_relief_to_recoverybclc.pdf.

Business Roundtable. 2006. About disaster response. *Partnership for disaster response.* http://www.respondtodisaster.com/mambo/index.php?option=com_content&task=section&id=11&Itemid=47.

Cabinet Office. 2002. *Disaster management in Japan* [in Japanese]. http://www.bousai.go.jp/index.html.

Center for Excellence in Disaster Management and Humanitarian Assistance. 2006. *Pakistan earthquake: A review of the civil-military dimensions of the international response.* http://64.233.167.104/search?q=cache:3nzB46AIldUJ:https://seneca.centcom.mil/humanitarian/documents/Pakistan_ERE//PAK%2520AAR%2520report%2520-FINAL%2520REPORT(2).doc+Pakistan+Earthquake:+A+Review+of+the+Civil-Military+Dimensions+of+the+International+Response&hl=en&ct=clnk&cd=2&gl=us.

Chikara Shima and Yuichi Obitsu. 2006. Government conducts large-scale anti-terror exercise. *Daily Yomiuri*, November 11.

China Post. 2009. Taiwan, Japan work to launch natural disaster relief platform. April 23. http://www.chinapost.com.tw/taiwan/foreign-affairs/2009/04/23/205438/Taiwan-Japan.htm.

Commission on the National Guard and Reserves. 2007. Strengthening America's defenses in the new security environment. Second report to Congress, March 1.

Congressional Research Service. 2005. Hurricane Katrina: DOD disaster response. Prepared by Steve Bowman, Lawrence Kapp, and Amy Belasco. CRS report to Congress, RL33095. September 19. http://www.fas.org/sgp/crs/natsec/RL33095.pdf.

———. 2006. The use of federal troops for disaster assistance: Legal issues. Prepared by Jennifer K. Elsea. CRS report to Congress, RS22266. Updated August 14. http://www.fas.org/sgp/crs/natsec/RS22266.pdf.

Council on Security and Defense Capabilities. 2004. The Council on Security and Defense Capability report –Japan's visions for future security and defense capabilities [in Japanese]. October. http://www.kantei.go.jp/jp/singi/ampobouei/dai13/13siryou.pdf.

Daily Yomiuri. 2004. Seven bills on foreign armed attack enacted. June 15.

———. 2006a. Nagaoka turns down donations for disasters. November 17.

———. 2006b. Takarazuka seeking disaster volunteers. December 28.

DefenseNews. 2007. Japan established rapid reaction force. March 28. http://www.defensenews.com/story.php?i=3450754.

DigitalGlobe. 2005a. DigitalGlobe satellite imagery helps relief workers in Indonesia establish refugee camps and medical reachback. News release. April 18. http://media.digitalglobe.com/index.php?s=press_releases&year=2005.

———. 2005b. DigitalGlobe's satellite imagery supports hurricane Katrina relief. News release. October 12. http://media.digitalglobe.com/index.php?s=press_releases&year=2005.

Eldridge, Robert D. 2006. U.S.-Japan bilateral cooperation in natural disasters. Presentation at IFPA-OSIPP 2006 workshop.

Fein, Geoff. 2006. Katrina showed need for rapid damage assessment, improved communications. *Defense Daily*, July 27.

Fox, Justin, 2005. Taking our chances: A meditation on risk. *Fortune* 152, no. 7 (Oct 3). http://money.cnn.com/magazines/fortune/fortune_archive/2005/10/03/toc.html.

GAO. 2006a. Hurricane Katrina: Better plans and exercises need to guide the military's response to catastrophic natural disasters. Statement for the Record to the Subcommittee on Terrorism, Unconventional Threats and Capabilities, Committee on Armed Services, House of Representatives. Prepared by Sharon Pickup, Director, Defense Capabilities and Management. GAO-06-808T, May 25. http://www.gao.gov/cgi-bin/getrpt?GAO-06-808T.

———. 2006b. Catastrophic disasters: Enhanced leadership, capabilities, and accountability controls will improve the effectiveness of the nation's preparedness, response, and recovery system. Report to Congressional Committees. GAO-06-618, September. http://www.gao.gov/cgi-bin/getrpt?GAO-06-618.

———. 2008. Preliminary observations on the progress and challenges associated with establishing the U.S. Africa Command. Testimony before the Subcommittee on National Security and Foreign Affairs, Committee on Oversight and Government Reform, House of Representatives. GAO-08-947T, July 15.

———. 2009. Actions needed to address stakeholder concerns, improve interagency collaboration, and determine full costs associated with the U.S. Africa Command. Subcommittee on National Security and Foreign Affairs, Committee on Oversight and Government Reform, House of Representatives. GAO-09-181. February.

Government of Japan and Government of the United States of America. 2004. *Agreement amending the agreement between the Government of Japan and Government of the United States of America concerning reciprocal provision of logistic support, supplies and services between the Self-Defense Forces of Japan and the Armed Forces of the United States of America.* February 27. http://www.mofa.go.jp/region/n-america/us/agree0403.pdf.

Gregson, Wallace C. 2009. Advance policy questions for Wallace C. Gregson: Nominee for Assistant Secretary of Defense for Asian & Pacific Security Affairs. http://hongkong.usconsulate.gov/uploads/images/lS35dbRF_Kq5O7nKjvtpeA/uscn_others_2009042801.pdf.

Hammerle, Hannelore, and Nicole Cremel. 2005. UNOSAT tackles tsunami challenge. *CERN Courier*, March 30. http://cerncourier.com/cws/article/cern/29295.

Hobson, Sharon. 2005. Disaster relief - Welcome relief? *Janes Defense Weekly,* May 18.

Hsu, Spencer S. 2005. Messages depict disarray in federal Katrina response. *Washington Post*, October 18.

IFPA-OSIPP. 2006. In times of crisis: Global and local civil-military coordination in the United States and Japan. Workshop organized by the Institute for Foreign Policy Analysis and the Osaka School of International Public Policy, Osaka University. Washington, D.C., December 12.

———. 2008. In Times of Crisis: U.S.-Japan Civil-Military Coordination for Disaster Relief Missions. Workshop organized by the Institute for Foreign Policy Analysis and the Osaka School of International Public Policy, Osaka University. Tokyo, Japan, October 28.

Inter-Agency Standing Committee. 2004. Civil-military relationship in complex emergencies. An IASC reference paper. June 28.

———. 2006. Real-time evaluation of the application of the cluster approach in the South Asia earthquake. February 10-20. http://www.unhic.org/documents/IASCEvaluationofClusterApproach-Pakistan%5BFINAL%5D.pdf.

interview. 2004. With high-ranking U.S. officer. August 2.

———. 2005. With U.S. NGO representative. September 7.

———. 2006a. With U.S. NGO representative. May 25.

———. 2006b. With UN OCHA official. November 10.

———. 2006c. With DoD official. November 13.

———. 2007a. With Japanese MOD official. March 19.

———. 2007b. With OFDA official. February 22.

Japan Association of Corporate Executives. 2004. Report of the Council on Iraqi Issues – Building a framework of new safety assurance and humanitarian and reconstruction assistance after warfare, formulating a general law and establishing 'Japanese CIMIC.' November.

Japan Defense Agency. 2006. *Defense of Japan 2006*. Fujisho: Yamagata.

JICA. 2008. Japan sends additional rescue workers to Chinese earthquake epicenter. May 16, 2008. http://www.jica.go.jp/english/resources/field/2008/may16. html.

———. 2009. *Facts and Figures*. http://www.jica.go.jp/english/news/field/2008/ pdf/081003.pdf.

Joshi, Vijay. 2008. Asia-Pacific eyes coordinated disaster relief work. Associated Press, July 24.

Kim Min-seok. 2008. Militaries of Japan, U.S., and Korea to cooperate. *JoongAng Daily*, February 20.

Kristof, Nicholas D. 2007. Aid workers with guns. *New York Times*, March 4.

Matthews, William. 2008. U.S. defense secretary seeks soft-power cadre. *Defense-News*, March 6.

Mercy Corps. 2007a. *2007 Annual report*. http://www.mercycorps.org/files/mc_ ar2007.pdf.

———. 2007b. Shifting from relief to recovery. March 21. http://www.mercycorps. org/countries/pakistan/917.

Miles, Donna. 2005. Joint Task Force Katrina established. American Forces Press Service. September 2. http://usmilitary.about.com/od/nationaldisasters/a/jtfka-trina.htm.

Ministry of Defense of Japan. 2008. *Defense of Japan 2008*. Urban Connections: Tokyo, Japan.

Ministry of Foreign Affairs of Japan. 1995. *National defense program outline in and after FY 1996*. http://www.fas.org/news/japan/ndpo.htm.

———. 2005. *U.S.-Japan Alliance: Transformation and realignment for the future*. Security Consultative Committee Document. October 29. http://www.mofa.go.jp/ region/n-america/us/security/scc/doc0510.html.

———. 2007. Japan-Australia joint declaration on security cooperation. March 13. http://www.mofa.go.jp/region/asia-paci/australia/joint0703.html.

————. 2008a. Joint declaration on security cooperation between Japan and India. October 22. http://www.mofa.go.jp/region/asia-paci/india/pmv0810/joint_d. html.

————. 2008b. *Emergency assistance for the cyclone disaster in the Union of Myanmar.* May 16. http://www.mofa.go.jp/announce/announce/2008/5/1180059_1010. html.

————. 2008c. *Cyclone disaster in Myanmar (return of Japan disaster relief medical team).* June 9. http://www.mofa.go.jp/announce/announce/2008/6/1180679_1020. html.

Ministry of Internal Affairs and Communication. 2008. *Statistical handbook of Japan 2008.* http://www.stat.go.jp/english/data/handbook/.

Nagamatsu Shingo. 2006. Development of CIMIC under the domestic disaster situations in Japan. Presentation at IFPA-OSIPP 2006 workshop.

National Journal's Congress Daily AM. 2005. Governors oppose expanding military's role in disasters. October 20.

New York Times. 2005. Re-examining the Red Cross. December 4.

Nippon Yusen Kaisha. 2006. NYK transports aid to earthquake-stricken areas of Pakistan. News release. July 26. http://www.nykline.co.jp/engliSH/info/2006/0726/ index.htm.

OCHA. 2007. *OCHA in 2007: Activities and extra-budgetary funding requirements.* Geneva: OCHA. http://ochaonline.un.org/webpage.asp?Page=2356.

————. 2009. *OCHA in 2009: Introduction and Financial Analysis.* Geneva: OCHA. http://ochaonline.un.org/ocha2009/intro-analysis.html.

PACOM. 2009. MPAT nations practice disaster relief procedures, improve regional disaster response in Philippines. *PACOM Blog,* April 5, 2009. http://us-pacific-command.blogspot.com/2009/04/mpat-nations-practice-disaster-relief.html.

People's Daily Online. 2008. Japan sends 800 more tents to China's quake-hit areas. June 4. http://www.english.people.com.cn/90001/90776/90883/6424438. html.

Perry, Charles M. 2009. *Finding the Right Mix: Disaster Diplomacy, National Security, and International Cooperation.* IFPA

Price, Jay. 2007. Stretched thin, 82nd Airborne giving up rapid-reaction unit. *Raleigh News & Observer,* March 22.

ReliefWeb. 2008. List of all humanitarian pledges, commitments and contributions in 2008. *China: earthquake in Sichuan Province – May 2008: Funding 2008.* http://www.reliefweb.int/rw/fts.nsf/doc105?OpenForm&rc=3&emid=EQ-2008-000062-CHN.

ROK Ministry of National Defense. 2009. Korea, Japan establish framework for military exchange. Press release. April 29. http://www.korea.net/news/news/news-View.asp?serial_no=20090429002&part=101&SearchDay=&page=1.

Schoff, James L., ed. 2004. *Crisis management in Japan and the United States: Creating opportunities for cooperation amid dramatic change*. Herndon, Virginia: Potomac Books.

———. 2005. *Tools for trilateralism: Improving U.S.-Japan-Korea cooperation to manage complex contingencies*. Herndon, Virginia: Potomac Books.

Terhune, Chad. 2005. Along battered Gulf, Katrina aid stirs unintended rivalry. *Wall Street Journal*, September 29.

Toy, Mary-Anne. 2008. Japan sends in military to help China. *The Age*, May 29.

Tyson, Ann Scott. 2005. Pentagon plans to beef up domestic rapid response forces. *Washington Post*, October 13.

UN. 1994. *Guidelines on the use of military and civil defense assets in disaster relief*. Geneva: UN. May. http://www.coe-dmha.org/Media/Guidance/2OsloGuidelines.pdf.

———. 2007. *Guidelines on the use of military and civil defense assets in disaster relief. "Oslo Guidelines."* Rev. 1. Geneva: UN. November. http://ochaonline.un.org/DocView.asp?DocID=5247.

———. 2008a. *Civil-military guidelines and reference for complex emergencies*. New York: UN OCHA. http://www.reliefweb.int/rw/lib.nsf/db900sid/ASIN-7CHT7T/$file/Full_Report.pdf?openelement

———. 2008b. *United Nations civil-military coordination officer field handbook*. Version E.1.1. Geneva: UN.

UN General Assembly. 1991. Strengthening of the coordination of humanitarian agency assistance of the United Nations. A/RES/46/182, 78th plenary meeting, December 19.

UN Development Program. Newsroom. 2005. UN signs disaster management partnership with DHL. December 15. http://content.undp.org/go/newsroom/un-dhl151205.en;jsessionid=axbWzt8vXD9?categoryID=349450&lang=en.

USAID. 2005. *Field operations guide for disaster assessment and response*. Vers. 4.0. http://www.usaid.gov/our_work/humanitarian_assistance/disaster_assistance/resources/pdf/fog_v4.pdf.

USAID OFDA. 2005. *Annual report for fiscal year 2005*. http://www.usaid.gov/our_work/humanitarian_assistance/disaster_assistance/publicationsannual_reports/index.html.

———. 2006. *Annual report for fiscal year 2006*. http://www.usaid.gov/our_work/humanitarian_assistance/disaster_assistance/publications/annual_reports/pdf/AR2006.pdf.

U.S. Department of Defense. 1993. Military support to civil authorities (MSCA). Directive 3025.1. Department of Defense Directive no. 3025.1, USD(P). January 15. http://www.dtic.mil/whs/directives/corres/pdf/302501_011593/302501p.pdf.

————. 2005. Military support for stability, security, transition, and reconstruction (SSTR). Directive 3000.05, USD(P). November 28. http://www.fas.org/irp/doddir/dod/d3000_05.pdf.

————. Security Cooperation Agency. 2006. Fiscal year (FY) 2007 budget estimates: Overseas humanitarian, disaster, and civic aid, defense (OHDACA). February. http://www.dod.mil/comptroller/defbudget/fy2007/budget_justification/pdfs/operation/O_M_VOL_1_PARTS/OHDACA.pdf.

U.S. Department of Homeland Security. 2004. *National Response Plan*. December. http://www.dhs.gov/xlibrary/assets/NRPbaseplan.pdf.

————. 2006. *National response plan*. May. http://www.dhs.gov/xprepresp/committees/editorial_0566.shtm.

————. 2008. National Response Framework. http://www.fema.gov/emergency/nrf.

U.S. Department of State and U.S. Agency for International Development. 2007. *Strategic plan fiscal years 2007-2012*. Washington, D.C. http://www.state.gov/documents/organization/86291.pdf.

U.S. Forces Japan. Fact sheet. http://www.usfj.mil/ (accessed April 2007).

U.S. House of Representatives. 2005. *Trouble exposed: Katrina, Rita, and the Red Cross: A familiar history*. An investigative report by the U.S. House Committee on Homeland Security Democratic Staff, prepared for Congressman Bennie G. Thompson.

————. 2006. *A failure of initiative: Final report of the Select Bipartisan Committee to Investigate the Preparation for and Response to Hurricane Katrina*. 109th Cong., 2nd sess. Washington, D.C.: GPO. February 15. http://a257.g.akamaitech.net/7/257/2422/15feb20061230/www.gpoaccess.gov/katrinareport/mainreport.pdf.

U.S. Joint Chiefs of Staff. 1996. *Interagency coordination during joint operations*. Vol. 1. Joint Publication 3-08. October 9.

————. 2006. *Interagency, intergovernmental organization, and nongovernmental organization coordination during joint operations*. Vol. 1. Joint Publication 3-08. March 17.

U.S. Northern Command. 2005a. Hard hats and helping hands. September 7. News release. http://www.northcom.mil/News/2005/090705d.html.

————. 2005b. U.S. Northern Command support to hurricane Katrina disaster relief. September 12. http://www.northcom.mil/News/2005/091205.html.

U.S. Senate. Committee on Foreign Relations. 2006. Embassies as command posts in the anti-terror campaign. Report to members of the Committee on Foreign Relations, United States Senate, 109th Cong., 2nd Sess. December 15. http://www.fas.org/irp/congress/2006_rpt/embassies.pdf.

U.S.-Japan Security Consultative Committee. 2007. Alliance transformation: Advancing United States-Japan security and defense cooperation. Joint statement. May 1. http://www.mofa.go.jp/region/n-america/us/security/scc/joint0705.html.

Vandiver, John. 2009. Projects reveal the high cost of poor coordination. *Stars and Stripes*, July 10.

Veillette, Connie. 2007. *Restructuring U.S. foreign aid: The role of the director of foreign assistance in transformational development.* A CRS report to Congress. Congressional Research Service. January 23. http://www.nationalaglawcenter.org/assets/crs/rl33491.pdf.

Watanabe Chisaki. 2007. Government estimate: 42,000 could die if big quake were to hit western Japan. *Daily Yomiuri Online*, November 1.

White House. 2005. Management of interagency efforts concerning reconstruction and stabilization. National security presidential directive 44 (NSPD-44). December 7. http://www.fas.org/irp/offdocs/nspd/nspd-44.html.

———. 2006. *The federal response to hurricane Katrina: Lessons learned.* February 23. http://www.whitehouse.gov/reports/katrina-lessons-learned/.

Yamaguchi Mari. 2007. Japan at higher risk of disaster amid aging, more skyscrapers and underground malls. *Daily Yomiuri Online*, June 1.

Yomiuri Shimbun. 2008a. Disaster relief team to take UN test. July 28.

———. 2008b. Japan, U.S. to review crisis plan. November 11.

Yoshizaki Tomonori. 2006. Japan's approach to civil-military coordination for overseas disasters. Presentation at IFPA-OSIPP 2006 workshop.

Acronyms and Abbreviations

AFRICOM	U.S. Africa Command
APHP	Asia-Pacific Humanitarian Partnership
ARF	ASEAN Regional Forum
ASDF	Air Self-Defense Forces (Japan)
ASEAN	Association of Southeast Asian Nations
CAP	Consolidated Appeals Process (United Nations)
CARE	Cooperative for Assistance and Relief Everywhere, Inc
CBRN	chemical, biological, radiological, and nuclear
CENTCOM	U.S. Central Command
CERF	Central Emergency Revolving Fund (United Nations)
CERN	European Organization for Nuclear Research
CGP	Center for Global Partnership, Japan Foundation
CIMIC	civil-military cooperation
CMCoord	civil-military coordination
CMCS	Civil-Military Coordination Section (United Nations)
CMO	civil-military operations
CMO	Office of Coalition and Multinational Operations (United States)
COCOM	combatant command
CRF	Central Readiness Force (Japan)
DAC	Disaster Assistance Center Pakistan
DART	Disaster Assistance Response Team (United States)
DCO	Defense Coordinating Officer (United States)
DFA	Director of Foreign Assistance (United States)
DHS	U.S. Department of Homeland Security
DoD	U.S. Department of Defense
DSCA	Defense Security Cooperation Agency (United States)

DSCA	Defense Support of Civil Authorities (United States)
ECHA	Executive Committee for Humanitarian Affairs (United Nations)
EMAC	Emergency Management Assistance Compact (United States)
EMT	Emergency Medical Technician
ERC	Emergency Relief Coordinator (United Nations)
ESF	emergency support function
FCSS	Field Coordination Support Section (United Nations)
FDMA	Fire Disaster Management Agency (Japan)
FEMA	Federal Emergency Management Agency (United States)
GDACS	Global Disaster Alert and Coordination System
GSDF	Ground Self-Defense Forces (Japan)
GSOMIA	General Security of Military Information
HA/DR	humanitarian assistance/disaster relief
HC	Humanitarian Coordinator (United Nations)
HDC	Headquarters for Disaster Countermeasures (Japan)
HSRT	Humanitarian, Stabilization & Reconstruction Team (United States)
IASC	Inter-Agency Standing Committee (United Nations)
ICRC	International Committee of the Red Cross
ICS	Incident Command System (United States)
ICVA	International Council of Voluntary Agencies
IDP	internally-displaced person
IFPA	Institute for Foreign Policy Analysis
IFRC	International Federation of Red Cross and Red Crescent Societies
IHP	International Humanitarian Partnership
INSARAG	International Search & Rescue Advisory Group
InterAction	American Council for Voluntary International Action
IOM	International Organization for Migration
IRIN	Integrated Regional Information Networks
JBIC	Japan Bank for International Cooperation
JDA	Japan Defense Agency
JDR	Japan Disaster Relief Teams
JDR Law	Law Concerning the Dispatch of Japan Disaster Relief Teams
JFO	Joint Field Office (United States)
JIACG	Joint Inter-Agency Coordination Group (United States)
JICA	Japan's International Cooperation Agency

J-Net	Japan Disaster Relief Network
JRCS	Japanese Red Cross Society
JTF	joint task force
LFA	Lead Federal Agency (United States)
LSU	Logistics Support Unit (United Nations)
MCAP	Multinational Cooperation in the Asia-Pacific (Japan)
MCDA	military or civil defense assets
MOD	Ministry of Defense (Japan)
MOFA	Ministry of Foreign Affairs (Japan)
MOU	memorandum of understanding
MPAT	Multinational Planning Augmentation Team
MSDF	Maritime Self-Defense Force (Japan)
NATO	North Atlantic Treaty Organization
NBC	nuclear, biological, chemical
NDPG	National Defense Program Guideline (Japan)
NGO	non-governmental organization
NIMS	National Incident Management System (United States)
NORTHCOM	U.S. Northern Command
NPA	National Police Agency (Japan)
NPO	non-profit organization
NRF	National Response Framework (United States)
NRP	National Response Plan (United States)
NSC	National Security Council (United States)
NSPD	National Security Presidential Directive (United States)
NVNAD	Nippon Volunteer Network Active in Disaster (Japan)
NVOAD	National Voluntary Organizations Active in Disaster (United States)
OCHA	UN Office for the Coordination of Humanitarian Affairs
ODA	overseas development and disaster assistance (Japan)
OFDA	Office of U.S. Foreign Disaster Assistance
OHCHR	Office of the High Commissioner for Human Rights (United Nations)
OLU	Operational Liaison Unit (United States)
OMA	Office of Military Affairs (United States)
OSD	Office of the Secretary of Defense
OSIPP	Osaka School of International Public Policy, Osaka University
OSOCC	On-site Operations Coordination Center (United Nations)

OUSD(P)	Office of the Under Secretary of Defense for Policy
PACOM	U.S. Pacific Command
PDD	Presidential Decision Directive
PFO	principal federal officer (United States)
PKO	Peacekeeping Operations
PWJ	Peace Winds Japan
RC	Resident Coordinator (United Nations)
RFA	request for assistance
RMT	Response Management Team (United Nations)
S/CRS	U.S. Office of the Coordinator for Reconstruction & Stabilization
SCC	Security Consultative Committee (United States-Japan)
SCHR	Steering Committee for Humanitarian Response
SDF	Self-Defense Forces (Japan)
SO/LIC	special operations/low-intensity conflict
SOUTHCOM	U.S. Southern Command
SSTR	Stability, Security, Transition, and Reconstruction
TRANSCOM	U.S. Transportation Command
TSC	theater security cooperation
UN	United Nations
UNDAC	UN Disaster Assessment and Coordination Team
UNDP	UN Development Program
UNHAS	UN Humanitarian Air Service
UNHCR	UN High Commissioner for Refugees
UNHRD	UN Humanitarian Response Depot
UNICEF	UN Children's Fund
UNJLC	UN Joint Logistics Centre
UNOSAT	Operational Satellite Applications Program (United Nations)
UNSAS	UN Stand-by Arrangement System
USAID	U.S. Agency for International Development
USFJ	U.S. Forces in Japan
USGS	United States Geological Survey
V-OSOCC	Virtual On-site Operations Coordination Center (United Nations)
WFP	World Food Program
WHO	World Health Organization
WMDs	weapons of mass destruction

About the Authors
and the Institute for
Foreign Policy Analysis

James L. Schoff is associate-director of Asia-Pacific Studies at the Institute for Foreign Policy Analysis, where he specializes in East Asian security and non-proliferation issues, international crisis management, and U.S. alliance relations in the region. Mr. Schoff has spent over twenty years working both in the private sector and the foreign policy research community on Asia-related issues, including five years living in Japan. He joined IFPA in 2003, after serving as the program officer in charge of policy studies at the United States-Japan Foundation. Recent publications include *Realigning Priorities: The U.S.-Japan Alliance & the Future of Extended Deterrence* (IFPA, 2009); *Nuclear Matters in North Korea: Building a Multilateral Response for Future Stability in Northeast Asia* (Potomac Books, 2008) (co-author); *Tools for Trilateralism: Improving U.S.-Japan-Korea Cooperation to Manage Complex Contingencies* (Potomac Books, 2005); and *Crisis Management in Japan and the United States: Creating Opportunities for Cooperation amid Dramatic Change* (Brassey's, 2004) (editor). Mr. Schoff graduated from Duke University and earned an M.A. in international relations at the Johns Hopkins University School for Advanced International Studies (SAIS). He also studied for one year at International Christian University (ICU) in Tokyo, Japan.

    Marina Travayiakis joined IFPA in 2006 as a research associate. Her research interests include post-conflict reconstruction and stabilization operations, civil-military coordination, and crisis management. Before joining IFPA, Ms. Travayiakis worked as a teaching assistant in the Department of Political Science at Tufts University. She also served as a research assistant at the Fletcher School at Tufts on a number of projects covering issues of transitional justice, democracy promotion, conflict management, and disarmament, demobilization and reintegration programs. Marina holds an M.A. in law and diplomacy from The Fletcher School, Tufts University, where she is currently enrolled as a Ph.D. Candidate.

The Institute for Foreign Policy Analysis (IFPA) is an independent, nonpartisan and not-for-profit (501(c)(3)) research organization that conducts research, publishes studies, convenes seminars and conferences, promotes education, and trains policy analysts in the fields of foreign policy and national security affairs. The institute maintains a staff of specialists at its offices in Cambridge, Massachusetts, and Washington, D.C. IFPA is associated with the Fletcher School, Tufts University. Since its founding in 1976, IFPA has provided a forum for the examination of political, economic, security, and defense-industrial issues confronting the United States in a rapidly changing world.